Poverty

ISSUES
(previously Issues for the Nineties)

Volume 9

Editor

Craig Donnellan

First published by Independence
PO Box 295
Cambridge CB1 3XP
England

British Library Cataloguing in Publication Data
Poverty– (Issues Series)
I. Donnellan, Craig II. Series
362.5

ISBN 1 86168 042 2

Printed in Great Britain
City Print Ltd
Milton Keynes

Typeset by
Claire Boyd

Cover
The illustration on the front cover is by
Andrew Smith.

CONTENTS

Chapter One: The Poverty Trap

Chapter Two: Global Poverty

Introduction

Poverty is the ninth volume in the series: **Issues**. The aim of this series is to offer up-to-date information about important issues in our world.

Poverty looks at poverty both in the UK and around the world.

The information comes from a wide variety of sources and includes:
Government reports and statistics
Newspaper reports and features
Magazine articles and surveys
Literature from lobby groups
and charitable organisations.

It is hoped that, as you read about the many aspects of the issues explored in this book, you will critically evaluate the information presented. It is important that you decide whether you are being presented with facts or opinions. Does the writer give a biased or an unbiased report? If an opinion is being expressed, do you agree with the writer?

Poverty offers a useful starting-point for those who need convenient access to information about the many issues involved. However, it is only a starting-point. At the back of the book is a list of organisations which you may want to contact for further information.

*****

Poverty

The facts

How many people live in poverty?

Poverty blights the lives of around a quarter of the UK's population and a third of its children. Latest figures show that between 13 and 14 million people were living in poverty in 1993/94.

The Low Income Families (LIF) statistics show that in the UK in 1992:

- 13,680,000 people – 24 per cent of the population of the UK – were living in poverty.
- Of these, 4,740,000 – 8 per cent of the population – were living below the poverty line. One of the principal reasons why people are living below the income support (IS) level is that they are not taking up means-tested benefits to which they are entitled; an estimated £2.2 – £3.5 billion of means-tested benefit went unclaimed in 1994/95.
- A total of 18,540,000 people – 33 per cent of the population – were living in or on the margins of poverty.
- The number of people in poverty has increased dramatically since 1979. In 1979 14 per cent of the population were living in poverty.

The Households Below Average Income (HBAI) statistics show similar levels of poverty in the UK in 1993/94 (Figures relate to the period April 1993-March 1995):

- 13.7 million people living in poverty – one quarter of the population.
- There has been a substantial increase in poverty since 1979 when 5 million – 9 per cent of the population – were living on incomes of below half the national average.

Some suggest that the vast numbers in poverty are due to over-generous poverty lines. The evidence suggests that the level of income measured by both poverty lines is unquestionably meagre in an affluent society.

Research which has looked at the cost of a modest-but-adequate lifestyle suggest that the 13-14 million people who are living in poverty according to either definition are forgoing many of the things that the rest of society takes for granted.

How many children?

- In 1993/94 there were 4.2 million children – one in three children – living in poverty according to the HBAI statistics. This compares to 1.4 million children (10 per cent) in 1979.
- According to the HBAI figures, children at greatest risk of poverty were those living in families where no one was in full-time work, particularly in large families. The risk of poverty was much lower for children in families where there was a full-time worker; nevertheless there was still an increased risk of poverty for large families.
- According to the LIF statistics in 1992 there were 3,690,000 children – 29 per cent of all children – living in poverty. Of these, 890,000 (6 per cent of children) were living in families with incomes below the Income Support poverty line.

Who is living in poverty?

The HBAI figures show that:

- The make-up of the poor since 1979 has changed; since 1979 the proportion of the poor who are lone parents, couples with children or single people has increased while the proportion who are pensioners has fallen.

- In 1993/94 couples with children accounted for the largest group in poverty – 36 per cent – followed by lone parents who make up 18 per cent of those in poverty.
- The risk of poverty is highest among the unemployed, people in families that only have access to part-time work and lone parent families.
- Unemployment accounts for more than a fifth of those living below 50 per cent of average income

Women in poverty outnumber men by about 1.2 million: the LIF statistics show that in 1992 approximately 5.4 million women were living in poverty compared to 4.2 million men. This is due to high levels of unemployment, low pay, women's unpaid work (including childcare responsibilities), poor distribution of resources within households and insufficient support via the social security system.

High levels of poverty are faced by many members of Black and minority ethnic groups. Unemployment rates for these groups are roughly twice that of white people and Black and minority ethnic employees are more likely to be low paid. Poverty among Black and minority ethnic groups is the result of immigration policy which has curtailed access to welfare services, inequalities in the labour market, society security policies which have been discriminatory and racism in society as a whole.

The causes of poverty

In the UK poverty is largely determined by three factors – access to the labour market, extra costs, and the overall failure of policies to deal with either of these.

Access to the labour market

- Levels of unemployment have remained high in the UK. There are well over 2 million un-employed people in 1996, over twice as many as there were in 1979. In 1994/95 170,000 families in Britain contained two or more unemployed people.
- Changes in the method of counting the unemployed have led to underestimation of the

number out of work – the Unemployment Unit estimates that unemployment is currently well over 3 million.

- Since 1986 the numbers of those who have lost their jobs and withdrawn from the labour market altogether have exceeded the numbers officially recognised as unemployed.
- The likelihood of unemployment is determined by social class, race and sex. In 1993 unemployment rates were three times as high for those in previously manual jobs as for those in non-manual employment.
- The number of long-term unem-ployed people has increased. In 1994 1.1 million people were long-term unemployed – 44 per cent of all unemployed people.
- Cuts to unemployment benefits since have contributed to rising levels of poverty among un-employed people.
- Disabled people are more likely to experience exclusion from the

labour market. The 1994/95 Family Resources Survey found that 48 per cent of households with a sick or disabled person received no income from employment.
- Poverty is also caused by low wages. In 1994, 37 per cent of full-time workers and 77 per cent of part-time workers were living on low pay, according to the Council of Europe's decency threshold (£221.50 a week or £5.88 an hour).

Extra costs
- Children bring extra costs for families. Between 1979 and 1993/94, the risk of poverty tripled among couples with children. In lone parent families the risk is particularly high; in 1993/94 59 per cent of people living in families headed by a lone parent were living in poverty, defined as below 50 per cent of average income after housing costs.
- Benefits do not meet extra costs. For example, child benefit has not been increased in line with costs; if child benefit had been uprated with inflation from 1979 onwards it would have stood at £10.85 for each child in April 1995. Its value fell by 4 per cent in real terms for the eldest child and 22 per cent for subsequent children.
- Disabled people also face

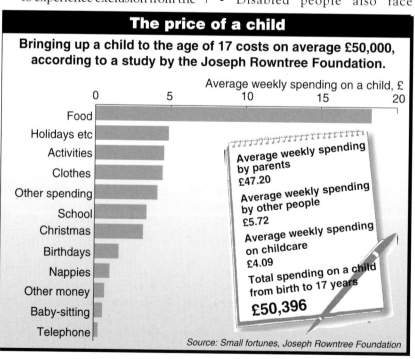

The price of a child

Bringing up a child to the age of 17 costs on average £50,000, according to a study by the Joseph Rowntree Foundation.

Average weekly spending on a child, £

Food, Holidays etc, Activities, Clothes, Other spending, School, Christmas, Birthdays, Nappies, Other money, Baby-sitting, Telephone

Average weekly spending by parents £47.20

Average weekly spending by other people £5.72

Average weekly spending on childcare £4.09

Total spending on a child from birth to 17 years £50,396

Source: Small fortunes, Joseph Rowntree Foundation

additional costs resulting from spending on items such as transport, heating, laundry, wear and tear on furniture and clothing, special diets, caring services and prescriptions. Cuts in benefits for disabled people have also led to an increase in levels of poverty.

- The costs of services, such as transport, day-care centres, meals-on-wheels and extra-curricular education charges have increased at a time when government subsidies have reduced.

The impact of poverty

Poverty filters into every aspect of life. It is not simply about doing without things; it is also about being denied the expectation of decent health, education, shelter, a social life, and a sense of self-esteem which the rest of society takes for granted.

- The 1995/96 Family Expenditure Survey showed that lone parents in the poorest fifth of the population spend £5.19 a week on leisure services compared to £32.05 in all households.
- CPAG's publication *Family Fortunes* shows that children from less affluent homes were much more likely to go on holiday in the UK rather than abroad; to have shorter holidays, and to be more dependent on day trips from school for their experience outside home than children from more affluent homes.
- In 1991, the NCH Action for Children's Poverty and Nutrition Survey found that one in five parents and one in ten children had gone without food in the previous month because they did not have enough money to buy food.
- Debt is a major cause of poverty in the UK. In 1994 133,700 homeowners were between 6-12 months in arrears with their mortgage payments compared to 42,810 in 1984. A Policy Studies Institute report found that a third of households with net weekly incomes of less than £100 had debts, compared with 2 per cent of households with incomes over £400 a week.
- Inequalities in health between

the rich and the poor extend throughout the lifespan. Life expectancy at birth is around seven years higher in Social Class I than in Social Class V and studies have shown growing inequalities in mortality rates relating to social class over recent years.

- The growth of homelessness over the 1980s and 1990s has been dramatic. In 1994 there were 122,660 homeless households compared to 55,530 in 1979. According to the 1991 Census 2,674 people were sleeping rough. This figure is generally regarded as a substantial underestimate – many rough sleepers are not easily visible.

The geography of poverty

- The scale and nature of poverty depend partly on where you live. Living standards are not evenly spread across the country, or within each city, town or village. There are large differences within regions. Extreme wealth and poverty can be seen in the South East, for example.
- Despite cosmetic gestures towards urban renewal, inner cities present some of the starker images of poverty. But poverty extends well beyond the towns and cities into rural areas. An estimated one-quarter of rural households live in or on the margins of poverty.

- A North-South divide persists, but it has been modified by the disproportionate impact of the early 1990s recession on the South East.
- Latest figures show that in 1988 52 million people – 15 per cent of the population – in the European Union were living in poverty.
- For one of the more prosperous countries of Europe, the UK has one of the highest rates of poverty. Between 1980 and 1988 the UK, along with Italy and Germany, experienced the sharpest rise in poverty.

The haves and the have nots

The gulf that has opened between poor and rich is clearly demonstrated by the Households below Average Income (HBAI) statistics. Over the last decade the living standards of the rich and poor have marched in opposite directions. Between 1979 and 1993/94 the poorest tenth of the population (including the self-employed) experienced a fall in their real income of 13 per cent compared to an average rise of 40 per cent for the whole of the population and a staggering leap of 65 per cent for the top tenth.

- Much of this information is taken from the newly updated version of *Poverty: the facts* by Carey Oppenheim and Lisa Harker, available by contacting CPAG. See page 41 for address details. © CPAG

The poverty debate

Information from Help the Aged

Elderly people are a section of the population traditionally seen as 'poor'. This perception has a potential impact on government policy: is the State Retirement Pension generous enough? What criteria should be used to uprate it? Should the State Retirement Pension remain the main source of income for elderly people, or should private provision (personal and occupational pensions) be encouraged?

There is, however, no agreement about how 'poverty' should be defined. In May 1989, John Moore, then secretary of State for Social Security, caused a furore by declaring that poverty in Britain no longer existed. He argued that absolute poverty, such as can be seen in developing countries, did not exist in Britain, and that for the 'poverty lobby' to insist that 'the rich are getting richer and the poor poorer' was to redefine 'inequality' as 'relative poverty'.

A second strand of argument is to ridicule the use of benefit levels as a measure of this 'relative poverty'. If people receiving Income Support are accounted 'poor', then each time benefit levels are increased, more people will fall below the threshold and be eligible to claim, and the more 'poor' people there will be. The Government's generosity, by this definition, is seen as creating poverty.

It should be remembered that the term 'retired population' spans an age range of 4 decades, from the early retired, fit person of 55 with a large occupational pension to a single woman of 85, surviving on Income Support. The 'retired population' is anything but homogeneous. However, despite these arguments, looking at the position of the retired population as a whole still gives the overall impression of a majority living on very limited means.

- In 1994, nearly, 1.6 million pensioners and their dependants in Great Britain were receiving Income Support payments. It has been estimated that between 810,000 to as many as 1.1 million pensioners may be eligible for Income Support, but are not claiming it. Moreover, around 1.4 million pensioner households (an estimated 2.3 million people?) not eligible for Income Support in 1994 still had sufficiently low incomes to qualify for Council Tax Benefit.
- In 1993/94, 24% of single pensioners and 22% of pensioner couples had incomes which were less than half average income. 71% of single pensioners and 64% of pensioner couples had incomes which were less than 80% of the average (*Households Below Average Income: a statistical analysis 1979-1993/94*, table F1(BHC)).
- Only one-third of people aged 65+ pay income tax (House of Commons Hansard, 11.06.93, col

364). This means that two-thirds (some 6 million people aged 65+) have an annual income of less than £5,090 (single people) or £12,546 (for a married couple).
- In MORI's 1990 survey on poverty in the UK for London Weekend Television's series *Breadline Britain 1990s*, retired people were one of the groups most likely to be 'poor'. MORI used a relative notion of 'poverty' in the survey, one based on a consensus. People not able to afford three or more items deemed necessities by a majority of those interviewed were classed as 'poor'.
- In the survey *Attitudes of Ageing*, produced by British Gas in 1991, 31% of pensioners said they sometimes struggled to pay for necessities.

Are retired people becoming better-off?

- The government has stated that since the 1970s, the income of pensioners has increased quite substantially in real terms, as the earnings of the working population have increased. The figures have been disputed, however, with others claiming that the real increase in pensioners' incomes has been small ('Pensioners' incomes and expenditure 1970-85', Dawson and Evans, *Employment Gazette* May 1987; and *Poverty in official statistics: two reports*, Johnson and Webb, Institute for Fiscal Studies 1990).
- Up to 1980, pensions were uprated annually by either the increase in prices (using the Retail Prices Index), or the increase in earnings, whichever was the greater. Since 1980, pensions have been uprated simply in line with the increase in the RPI. This

has resulted in the basic rate pension for a couple dropping from 31.5% of average male earnings in 1979 to 24.7% of average male earnings in 1991 (Disney and Whitehouse, Fiscal Studies, 12(3), August 1991). Had the link with the increase in earnings been maintained, the basic pension in 1993/94 would be worth £18.45 more for a single person and £29.50 more for a couple (Hansard, 6.12.93, col 112).

Moreover, the RPI measures the price of goods and services used by the 'average family'. Pensioner households are not 'average families'. A single pensioner household, relying mainly on state benefits, spends a considerably higher proportion of income on essentials like food and fuel than the average family does: 26.5% of income on food, compared with 18.2%, and 11.4% on fuel, compared with 4.5%

A single pensioner household, relying mainly on state benefits, spends a considerably higher proportion of income on essentials like food and fuel than the average family does

(Family Spending 1995-1996, tables 1.1 and 4.1). Any rise in the cost of these essentials (for example through the recent imposition of VAT on domestic fuel) will therefore affect single older people far more than the RPI implies.

- Occupational pensions are said to be making a great difference to pensioners' incomes, as more and more people are retiring with more than the state pension: in 1990/91, 61% of pensioner households had income from occupational pensions. However, the average amount received from these pensions was £60.80 a week; that is just over £3,000 a year. Moreover, although recently retired households do have higher occupational pensions than the average pensioner household, the difference is not large: an average of £71.60 per week as opposed to £60.80 (Pensioner Income Results 1979-1990/91, DSS, table 3)

- The dramatic rise in property prices during most of the 1980s is also said to have greatly increased the assets of retired home owners. Although commercial 'equity-release' schemes do exist, they are not always an appropriate option, leaving the problem of the 'house-rich, cash-poor' elderly home owner.

© Help the Aged

Children caught in poverty trap

By Michael Streeter

Children are suffering the most from the growing gap between rich and poor in Britain, which is helping to make the role of social workers almost impossible, according to a leading academic.

Professor Jane Lewis, a fellow of All Souls College, Oxford, claims the growth in child poverty is so serious it means Britain will have difficulty implementing Article 27 of the United Nations Convention on the Rights of the Child. This concerns the 'right of children to a standard of living adequate for children's physical, mental, spiritual, moral and social development'.

Professor Lewis, director of the Wellcome Unit for the History of Medicine, and writing in *Community Care* magazine on the day that the Rikki Neave report was published,

says social workers were having to pick up the pieces from other parts of the welfare state.

She said that the rising number of children excluded from school and the greater number of sick people cared for by social services rather than by the medical profession meant social services were 'very much the end of the line'. Social work was always difficult in a liberal democracy, when social controls conflict with personal freedoms, writes Professor Lewis, 'but in such a profoundly unequal society their role becomes the well-nigh impossible one of containment.'

She adds: 'More oppressive poverty means social problems will be manifested in more worrying ways.'

Professor Lewis also attacks politicians for failing to tackle social

problems affecting children. She says: 'The statistics on child poverty have been reasonably well-publicised, as have been the shocking outcomes for a high percentage of children in care. But there is no sign of any political party wholeheartedly embracing the language of investment in children. Calls for containment and control are much more prevalent.'

In her wide-ranging article on the state of community care, Professor Lewis calls for a change in tone and content of debate, to re-invent the language of 'trust, mutual aid, co-operation and citizenship' against the current tone of consumerism and private responsibility.

© *Independent*
January, 1997

Poverty and financial security

Information from the Fawcett Society

Women and poverty in the 90s

'*Poverty must be the top priority for Government*'

In 1990/91 research found that over 4.6 million women had independent incomes of less than £25 a week compared with 0.4 million men.

The majority of women earn less and own less in their own right than men. At the age of 30 most women are still mainly dependent on the income of their partner, or the state if they do not have a partner. Two groups of women are particularly vulnerable, women with children, especially lone mothers, and lone older women, especially widows and divorced women.

Counting women in – understanding the poverty of women

'*Father had the money, mother had none . . . He never gave her a penny.*'

In two 1996 studies analysing poverty in the UK, one excluded two-thirds of women of working age and all pensioners, and the other excluded data about women completely.

In studies of poverty and wealth women are often ignored, or subsumed within the household, because it makes analysis of the data much simpler. However, when a Rowntree study looked at the income of women they found that women's contribution to the household was crucial in keeping low income families above poverty thresholds.

Since most women both earn less and own less than most men, policy makers must consider the different outcomes of their proposals on women as well as men.

Policy change – to introduce a system to analyse the annual Govern-ment budget proposals for their impact on women and men and publish a budget gender impact statement.

It is also important not to assume

Information from the Fawcett Society

equal sharing of income within households. Studies of the management of money within the home have found income and assets in the majority of households are not shared equally.

Policy change – to provide funding for research into how incomes are split within households to allow planners to understand the long-term impact of low independent incomes on women.

Why are women low-paid workers?

'*I want a wage that does not need supplementing with family credit*'

2.3 million people earn less than £3.50 an hour. Three-quarters of them are women.

Women form the majority of low-paid workers. Part-time workers

---

are likely to be low paid and many black women earn less than white women. The undervaluing of work done by women is one reason for women's low pay.

Another key factor is the weaker bargaining power of women in the labour market. For many women, the choice is low income or no income.

As well as being less likely to benefit from Trade Union support, women have limited access to state benefits (only 2% receive unemployment benefit), especially if they have an earning partner or children or earn below the National Insurance threshold. The greater the need of women, the more difficult it is for them to bargain for higher wages as they fear losing their jobs altogether.

Policy change – to introduce a minimum wage of not less than £3.50 an hour to put a floor under wages.

Nearly 3 million women earn less than the lower earnings threshold for National Insurance (£61). They do not contribute to the NI system and are therefore excluded from the benefits.

A combination of low pay and part-time work keeps many people, mainly women, below the earnings threshold for National Insurance. A growing number of people have a combination of part-time jobs, each below the threshold, although their total weekly wage is above. Setting a NI threshold encourages employers to keep wages and hours below the threshold limits.

Those outside the NI system are not entitled to unemployment benefit, statutory sick pay or maternity pay. Unless they have children under 16 they are also denied state pension credits.

Policy change – to revise the NI system to ensure that all adult earners are included.

Women's caring responsibilities and financial security

'Why should I be poor just because I am a mother?'
Couples with children are twice as likely to have a lower than average income than couples without children. Half of all single mothers are in the lowest income bracket.

Most couples suffer a drop in earnings when they have children at a time when their living costs increase. When children are born, around one-third of women stop earning and a further third switch to part-time work. Most of these women never recover their former earning level.

A study of women aged 30 found that for 65% of women not in paid employment their only direct income was Child Benefit. This important allowance plays a key role in helping women with low incomes to supplement and plan their household budgets.

Policy change – to increase Child Benefit, as an alternative to the present married couples' allowance. Entitlement to Child Benefit should be universal for all parents, including refugees and asylum seekers.

Lone parents are most likely to be living in poverty. Their situation is summed up by Carey Oppenheim, 'The problems of managing on a single wage, very often at low levels, with little access to affordable childcare, means that many lone mothers find themselves forced to rely on means-tested benefits for long periods'.

Women and the welfare benefit system

'I want a way out of the benefit trap'
Women whose partners become unemployed are likely to leave paid work themselves. A division is arising between two-earner and no-earner households.

The inflexibility of the benefits system leads many women whose partners are unemployed also to leave the labour market. When the period for unemployment benefit ends and means-tested benefits begin, every pound earned is a pound taken off income support. Income support is not available at all to those working over 16 hours per week.

In addition, when women themselves become unemployed they often do not qualify for unemployment benefit (now called the Job Seeker's Allowance) and if they have an earning partner they will not qualify for income support.

Policy change – to remove the 16-hour rule and other benefit traps which keep the spouses of unemployed people out of the labour market and restore the entitlement period for Job Seeker's Allowance to one year.

Why are women poor in old age?

'Because I had to give up my career to care for my children I have no pension'
The average occupational pension among women is £30 per week compared with £61 for men.

Women are more likely than men to suffer poverty in old age. They have not been able to build up an adequate income for their retirement. This is the effect of a lifetime of low earnings or no earnings and periods out of the labour

---

By the year 2000 the state pension will be worth so little that everyone will need a second pension

---

market caring for families. It is especially damaging to the build-up of private pensions.

Most women are dependent on their partner's pension and when the man dies the value of these can be drastically cut, often to less than half the original pension income. This leaves women heavily dependent on state benefits such as income support or living just above income support level by eking out their savings.

Policy change – to ensure a minimum pension income in retire-ment above income support level and to introduce a flexible decade of retirement starting from the age of sixty for both women and men.

At present only 1 in 5 women qualify for a full state pension. This situation is changing and by the year 2020 most women will qualify for a full state pension. By that time the state pension will be worth so little that everyone will need a second pension.

Policy change – to ensure that any additional pension schemes give women an equal chance to build up adequate provision.

Action on women and poverty

We want the Government to:
- Analyse its budget proposals for their impact on women
- Research the way income is split between men and women in households
- Introduce a minimum wage of not less than £3.50 per hour
- Revise the NI system to ensure all adult earners are included
- Increase Child Benefit
- Remove the 16-hour rule and other benefit traps
- Ensure a minimum pension income in retirement

What can you do?

Join Fawcett and help campaign against poverty among women. Fawcett is at the leading edge of campaigning for women in Britain today. Our many supporters, both women and men, are working for a society in which women and men are equal partners. Your support for Fawcett will give women a stronger voice – for ourselves, our daughters and our grand-daughters.

© Fawcett Society

Life on a low income

Information from the Joseph Rowntree Foundation

One in four of the British population live in homes with less than half the average disposable income. A special report by Elaine Kempson of the Policy Studies Institute looks behind the income and wealth statistics and draws on 31 recent research studies to explore what life on a low income is really like in the 1990s. It concludes that:

- People who live on low incomes are not an underclass with different attitudes and values to the rest of society. They aspire to a job, a decent home and an income that will cover their outgoings with a little to spare.
- Most are resourceful in trying to make ends meet, but those living on the lowest incomes – including social security benefits – face invidious choices between cutting back on essentials or falling into debt.
- An additional £15 a week would greatly improve the ability of people on very low incomes to cope. Had the link between earnings and the indexation of social security payments not been broken in the early 1980s, many of today's claimants would have the extra money they need to avoid real hardship.
- Low-income households frequently fall behind with basic household bills such as rent, mortgage, gas, electricity, water and Council Tax. Most people feel ashamed of their debts, but their situation is one of 'can't pay' rather than 'won't pay.'
- Chronic financial difficulties place strains on low-income households that often prove damaging to mental and physical health and to family relationships.
- Parents are determined to provide the best food and clothing that they can for their children, even when it means going without themselves.
- Women, who normally manage family budgets, adopt such strategies as frequent shopping to minimise food stocks at home and shopping without children or partners to avoid pressure to spend more.
- Finding a job is the only way that most people on benefits believe they can secure an adequate income. Yet individuals often alternate between unemployment and low-paid work in a way that offers no real escape from life on a low income.

> *Most people feel ashamed of their debts, but their situation is one of 'can't pay' rather than 'won't pay'*

Background

In 1995 the Joseph Rowntree Foundation Inquiry into Income and Wealth reported on social and economic changes that have produced increasing polarisation between a prosperous majority and a growing minority of people living on low incomes. Between 1979 and 1993 the number of individuals living in households with less than half the average net income (after housing costs) grew from 5 million to 14 million – including more than 4 million children. Among these low-income households are 9.8 million people who live on the benefit 'safety net' provided by Income Support.

Setting aside the debate about whether these measures define a poverty line, the present report explores what life is really like in the mid-1990s for people whose incomes are low. It also considers how particular social, economic and policy changes have affected their lives. The report reaches its conclusions by drawing on 31 recent

research studies whose in depth 'qualitative' methods allowed people living on low incomes to speak for themselves.

Making ends meet

'I've got to put my money away for bills before I can relax and even think about food.'

People living on low incomes often show great resilience in trying to make ends meet. Some find that managing the household budget is almost a full-time occupation. But while there are those who do not organise their affairs so carefully, there is scant evidence that they are reckless. The research suggests that most learn through trial and error, so that those who have lived on low incomes for longer tend to be more successful at making ends meet. Many families appear to plan their spending in detail, while a minority operate a pay-as-you-go approach. But even the most careful budgeting system can break down when money is tight. No matter how resourceful, those living on social security benefits generally find that no amount of forward planning and bill juggling is enough. They face a difficult choice between cutting back drastically on food, fuel and other essentials or falling into debt.

Going without

'When you're pushing the trolley around and you see people pushing one that's almost full and yours isn't, I think "I wish I could just put what I wanted in and not have to worry, but I can't."'

Surviving on a low income means going without. So men, who normally manage family budgets, resort to strategies that include frequent shopping to keep any food stocks at home to a minimum, systematic searching for special offers and shopping without children or partners to avoid pressure to spend more. Anxiety to avoid waste leads some mothers to buy convenience foods that they know their children will eat, even though they are not conducive to a healthy diet. But while families on very low incomes generally have poorer diets than those who are better off, parents struggle hard to ensure their children

Average spending on children

Weekly and from birth to 17 years, the spending on children by parents, other people and the costs of childcare.

Per week	
Parents	£47.20
Childcare	£4.09
Other people	£5.72
Total	**£57.01**

Birth to 17 years	
Parents	£41,724.80
Childcare	£3,615.56
Other people	£5,056.48
Total	**£50,396.84**

Source: Joseph Rowntree Foundation, Findings 118, 07/97

do not go without and that their lunch boxes are as well filled as those of their classmates. Parents in a wide range of research studies were adamant that they would not compromise on spending on their children even if it meant going without themselves. Although parents might economise on clothes for themselves, they were concerned to buy the best affordable quality for their children – often using mail-order catalogues to spread the cost.

Incurring debt

'You feel degraded. You think other people know that you are in debt. You think you have done something wrong.'

Low-income households frequently fell behind with their bills – rent, mortgage, gas, electricity, water and Council Tax – rather than the consumer credit arrears accumulated by better-off debtors. These types of debt carry the harshest sanctions in terms of repossession, disconnection, fines and even imprisonment. The research suggests that most people are ashamed of being in debt and that the unsympathetic practices of some creditors cause them added anxiety. For those whose homes are repossessed the sense of public humiliation appears especially strong. The great majority of those who owe money on major household bills acknowledge their debt and their obligations to creditors. Their situation is, therefore, one of 'can't pay' rather than 'won't pay'. Families with children in the research studies tended to have higher arrears than other households. Parents whose children needed something they could not really afford described how

they had borrowed or even delayed paying bills in order to find the money.

Impact on family life

'Little things that never mattered before are suddenly major issues and you fight over them. I fight with him [her husband], I shout at the kids, he does as well and the kids cry.'

Financial difficulties mean many people lose contact with their friends, lead restricted social lives, and spend a lot of time at home with their families. This can cement family relationships but more often it places a strain on them. In extreme cases the result can be family breakdown. However, the research suggested that men, women and children tended to feel the stresses of life on a low income in different ways:

Men who were unemployed or unable to learn a decent wage described feelings of worthlessness at no longer being a family 'breadwinner'. Older men and those who had been in better-paid, white-collar jobs were especially hard hit. ('I'm too old at 40. Ready for the heap. It's terrible.')

Women tended to bear the brunt of trying to make the available money go as far as possible. They shopped around for cheap food and clothing and were the family member most likely to make sacrifices for their children. ('I cook a meal and as long as there's plenty for them, I make do with a piece of toast.')

Children felt the stigma of coming from a low-income family in spite of their parents' best efforts to protect them from teasing and bullying. ('Sometimes they say: "Look at the horrible clothes he's got on. I'm not playing with you, you look horrible."')

Poor health

'What has happened to me now is that I'm so fed up of the whole situation; I think I've lost interest.'

Poor diet, inadequate housing, job insecurities and money worries appear to be part of the link between low income and a greater likelihood of ill health. People on low incomes tend to have diets that are low in fresh fruit and high in fat. Chronic illness may, in turn, be exacerbated by difficulties in affording extra heating or a special diet. The stress and despair associated with life on a low income leads some to become deeply depressed and, in a few extreme cases, to suicide.

Finding work

'There's a certain amount of work here and those that are unemployed are unemployed.'

Most people view a job as the only way they can secure an adequate income. The research makes it clear that they do not want to be dependent on the state and would prefer to provide for themselves and their families through a 'living wage'. Many go to great lengths to find a job, especially if they are the main breadwinner. But the market for unskilled and semi-skilled workers has contracted rapidly, adding to chronic, long-term unemployment. Low-skilled men tend to marry low-skilled women resulting in a growing polarisation between households with two wage-earners and those with none.

Most people who lose their jobs do not stay out of work for very long, but the research reveals how individuals can alternate between unemployment and low-paid work in a way that offers no real escape from life on a low income. Would-be

---

The stress and despair associated with life on a low income leads some to become deeply depressed and, in a few extreme cases, to suicide

---

workers are expected to take a flexible approach to the job market, accepting casual and low-paid, short-term jobs. Yet the inflexibility of the social security system means that those who take them benefit very little financially unless they fail to disclose them and commit fraud.

Incentivising wage levels

'There's no job that'll pay me enough to keep on top. There's so much I have to pay.'

The research demonstrates that unemployed people's wage aspirations are generally modest. Typically they say they need £20 to £30 on top of their weekly outgoings to relieve the worries and deprivations that characterise their lives. This implies a net weekly income of:
- £150 for single householders

- £175 for couples without children

- £180 for a lone parent with two children

- £200 for couples with two or three children

Current wage levels are often too low to meet these aspirations. In-work benefits such as Family Credit can be used to make low-paid jobs more attractive, but make it difficult for claimants to increase their incomes through additional work. In practice, a combination of in-work benefits and a national minimum wage, in conjunction with adjustments to tax, National Insurance and Child Benefit levels may prove the most viable way of ensuring adequate income in work.

Further information

The full report, *Life on a Low Income* by Elaine Kempson, is published for the Joseph Rowntree Foundation by York Publishing Services Ltd, 64 Hallfield Road, Layerthorpe, York YO3 7XQ Tel: 01904 430033 (price £9.50 plus £1 p&p)

• The above article is an extract from *Life on a Low Income, Findings Social Policy Research 97*, produced by the Joseph Rowntree Foundation. See page 41 for address details.

© Joseph Rowntree Foundation
June, 1996

Childhood poverty and parents' work

A nationally representative survey of British children has been carried out by the Centre for Research in Social Policy at Loughborough University. The study defined more than one in ten children as 'poor' if they do not have three or more necessities because their parents cannot afford to buy them. Three per cent of children are defined as 'severely poor' because they go without five or more necessities.

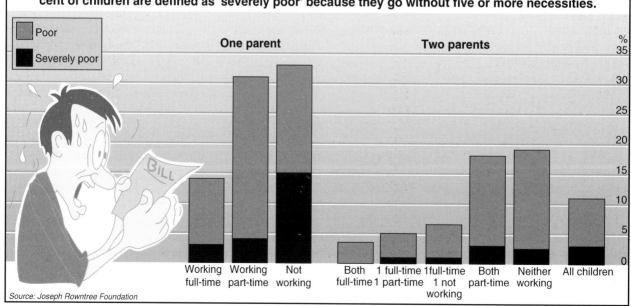

Source: Joseph Rowntree Foundation

Poverty and the minimum wage

Low pay is the single most important cause of poverty in Britain. A third of those defined as poor are in families where someone works, in many cases where they are employed full time. It is often argued by Ministers that a minimum wage would do little or nothing to help the poor, since most of those on a low income are dependent on social security. However, the government's own figures give the lie to this assertion.

According to the latest DSS figures (1993), of the 14.1 million people in poverty, at least 4.6 million (31.1 per cent) have an income from employment. This includes the self-employed, but by no means all of these are accountants and journalists fallen on hard times. Many are home-workers or other groups classified by their employer as 'self-employed' so as to avoid paying national insurance contributions or being liable for employment rights. As the Joseph Rowntree Inquiry found 'the low income self-employed (are) disproportionately female, young, working in areas like "personal and protective services" or as "labour only" sub-contractors'. Even if we exclude them from the calculation, over twenty per cent of the poor are in households where someone works, a total of 3.1 million people. In two out of three cases, the household has an income from full-time employment, but is still amongst the poor. So the 'working poor' now represent a bigger group than the unemployed or pensioners amongst the poor. Indeed, many of those aged over 60 and classified as having a low income will still be in work.

It is often argued that there is little overlap between family poverty and low pay because most of the low paid are women, who are not the main 'breadwinners'. Yet in the growing number of single-parent families, women are the only wage-earner. Many more households depend on having two earners to avoid poverty. The proportion of women in paid work increased fastest during the 1980s in households where their partner was low paid. Without the additional earnings of women workers, the numbers in poverty would increase by up to 50%. While the pooling together of low earnings in a household may disguise the effect of poverty pay, it does not eradicate it.

Low pay has a clear direct effect in generating poverty and hardship. But it also has an indirect effect. There is no automatic link between poverty and old age. Nor is there an inevitable link between unemployment and poverty: witness the living standards of many senior executives who lose their jobs through incompetence or company mergers. The reason why many people face poverty during periods of sickness or unemployment and during their retirement is that their earnings while at work have been insufficient to tide them over these periods.

Some argue that the problems of the 'working poor' should be dealt with through social security, rather than through a minimum wage. But this makes the poverty trap worse. Already, low earners in receipt of Family Credit and housing benefit stand to gain only 3p out of each extra pound they earn. While the rich face a maximum tax rate of 40p in the pound, the poorest lose up to 97p in the pound.

Most people want a decent wage for the work they do, without having to rely on social security benefits to bring their wages up to an adequate level. Currently, the taxpayer spends almost £2.5 billion in social security to subsidise low-paying employers by topping up the wages of their staff with social security.

Even with a minimum wage of £4 an hour, a family with children is ensnared in the poverty trap. Setting the minimum at a lower level would leave many families trapped even more deeply in the mire of taxes and means-tested benefits.

© Low Pay Unit
November, 1997

Who are the poor?

Over twenty per cent of the poor are in households where someone works, a total of 3.1 million people. In two out of three cases, the household has an income from full-time employment, but is still amongst the poor.

Type of household	Numbers (Millions)	Percentage
Self-employed	1.5	10.6
Single or couple in full-time work	0.3	2.1
One working full-time, one part-time	0.3	2.1
One working full-time, one unemployed	1.3	9.2
One or more in part-time work	1.2	8.5
Aged over 60	3.3	23.4
Unemployed	3.1	22.0
Others	3.1	22.0
Total	14.1	100.0

Source: DSS Households below average income 1979-1992/3

Millions would benefit from £4 minimum wage

By Larry Elliott, Economics Editor

Four and a half million low-paid workers will receive a pay rise if Britain's big unions achieve their aim of a national minimum wage set at £4.42 an hour, according to Government figures released yesterday. Figures from the Office for National Statistics show that 21 per cent of the country's 21.5 million employees would benefit from a pay floor set at half male median earnings.

Almost half of Britain's six million part-time workers earn less than £4.42 an hour, while one-seventh of all full-time employees are also paid less than the figure sought by unions such as Unison, which represent large numbers of the low paid.

The Low Pay Commission – the tripartite body set up by the Government to recommend a level for the statutory minimum wage – is unlikely to come up with a figure as high as £4.42 an hour. But the ONS numbers indicate that a pay norm set at slightly lower levels would still affect millions of workers.

The ONS said that 14.4 per cent of all employees earned less than £4 an hour, 7.6% less than £3.50 an hour, 2.8% less than £3 an hour and 1.5% less than £2.50 an hour.

Union leaders have tried to keep their bargaining position open, but are looking for at least £4 an hour, a figure which would boost the earnings of almost 40 per cent of part-time workers, most of whom are women. While 8.4 per cent of full-time employees are paid less than £4 an hour, 36.9 per cent of part-time workers are on less than this figure. In the North-east, 48.3 per cent of part-timers take home less than £4 an hour, and 58.3 per cent earn less than £4.42 an hour.

A regional breakdown shows Wales with the highest proportion of full-time employees earning below £2.50 (1.1 per cent) while London had the lowest at 0.5 per cent. In some London constituencies – Bexleyheath, Fulham and Islington North – there were no full-time workers earning under £4 an hour.

Scotland had the highest concentration of part-time employees on less than £2.50 an hour (5.5 per cent) and Merseyside the lowest (3.2 per cent). St Ives in Cornwall, with a high proportion of seasonal workers, had almost one-third of employees on less than £4 an hour, the highest figure anywhere in Britain.

London's reputation as an area of higher employment, higher living costs and higher wages was reflected by the ONS breakdown. Just 3.3 per cent of full-time workers in the capital earn less than £4 an hour, compared with a national average of 8.4 per cent. One in nine full-time employees in Wales and one in ten in Scotland were earning less than £4 an hour, according to the figures.

Separate figures released by the ONS today show that just under 20 per cent of households lacked a worker in employment in the spring of last year, a sharp rise from the 16 per cent recorded between 1984 and 1991. Employment minister Andrew Smith said the trend presented Labour with one of its most serious challenges.

© The Guardian
September, 1997

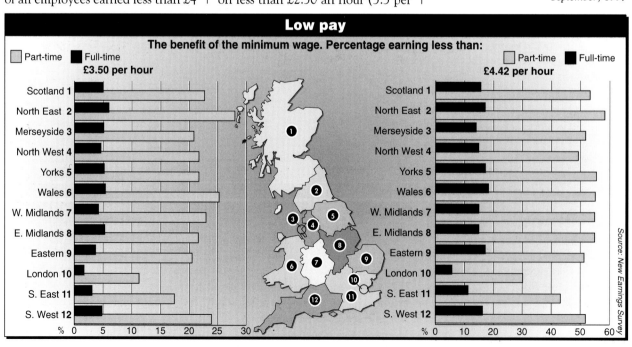

Low pay

The benefit of the minimum wage. Percentage earning less than:

Source: New Earnings Survey

Wales 'the poor relation' of UK

By David Gow

Scotland enjoys a far greater share of public spending and has seen rapidly increasing prosperity over the past 20 years, while its devolution partner, Wales, has got poorer as its subsidies from London have stagnated, it emerged yesterday.

On the eve of today's Scots referendum on setting up an Edinburgh parliament with tax-varying powers, the Institute of Welsh Affairs added weight to the campaign to slash fiscal transfers to Scotland with fresh evidence that Wales has become Britain's poorest region and its Celtic cousin one of the richest.

A report for the institute by two senior economists at Bangor University, Ross MacKay and Rick Audas, argues that the formula for allocating shares of public spending to England, Scotland and Wales should be drastically revised, with or without devolution.

The Barnett formula, drawn up in 1978 by the then Labour Treasury chief secretary, Joel (now Lord) Barnett, in the run-up to the first devolution referendums a year later, allocated 'identifiable' government spending to the three nations of Britain on a ratio of 85 for England, 10 for Scotland and five for Wales. Five years ago it was marginally adjusted to 85.7; 9.14; 5.16.

But the authors argue that 20 years ago Scottish output (GDP) per head was about 86 per cent of the UK average while fiscal transfers amounted to about 10 per cent of GDP. By 1994/95 Scottish output was equal to the UK average while the transfers remained constant in real terms.

In Wales, by contrasts, GDP per head fell in the same period from 88 to 83 per cent of the UK average, while fiscal transfers did not increase to reflect that growing gap. 'The scale

of transfer to Wales has not increased in spite of decline in relative prosperity,' the authors say.

Their evidence shows that household income in Wales is 14 per cent below the UK average, average full-time earnings 10 per cent below and activity rates (people actively employed) 8 per cent below. Scotland, on most criteria, ranks among the top three or four of Britain's 11 regions.

Even so, identifiable government spending per head in Scotland was £4,505 in 1995 compared with £4,208 in Wales – and £3,604 in England. Similarly, 46 per cent of Scotland qualifies for maximum regional grants while, since 1993,

the parts of Wales that qualify have slumped from 35 to 15 per cent.

Brian Morgan, of the Cardiff business school, concluded in the report that a Welsh assembly should negotiate a better and more transparent set of formulas for resource allocation and link these more closely to relative economic prosperity.

Mr Morgan also argued that it was in the Welsh interest that the assembly have no tax-varying powers, as introducing regional taxes would reduce investment.

• *The Economic Impact of a Welsh Assembly*, Institute of Welsh Affairs, Llandaf, Caerdydd. CF5 2YQ

© *The Guardian*
September, 1997

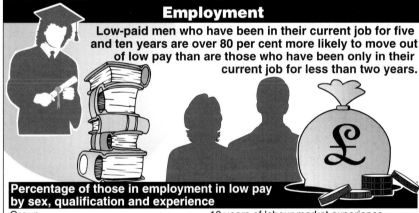

Employment

Low-paid men who have been in their current job for five and ten years are over 80 per cent more likely to move out of low pay than are those who have been only in their current job for less than two years.

Percentage of those in employment in low pay by sex, qualification and experience

Group		10 years of labour market experience			
		Direct job changes		Out of work between jobs	
	Entering labour market for first time tenure	Move at 5 years, 5 years tenure	Move at 10 years, 0 years tenure	Move at 5 years, 5 years tenure	Move at 10 years, 0 years tenure
Men	%	%	%	%	%
No qualifications	41.8	3.8	3.8	6.8	10.0
School only qualifications	33.3	4.0	4.2	7.2	6.6
Other further qualifications	15.7	1.6	1.6	3.3	3.7
College qualifications	3.4	1.0	1.0	1.7	1.7
Women	%	%	%	%	%
No qualifications	35.6	13.7	19.4	20.9	21.2
School only qualifications	35.7	6.3	8.3	17.6	13.2
Other further qualifications	21.4	3.8	9.6	7.8	13.7
College qualifications	8.2	0.7	1.3	3.3	4.4

Source: Joseph Rowntree Foundation

The children of poverty

One child in ten is living in poverty, an influential research group claimed yesterday.

A survey by the Rowntree Foundation found that it costs £3,000 a year to bring up a child in Britain and that parents on low incomes make big sacrifices for their children.

It also said benefits were too low to cover the cost of children for unemployed parents. But the findings for the foundation, which has regularly commissioned work that says poverty is widespread and worsening, ran against recent claims by poverty lobby organisations that one child in three can be considered poor. Critics challenged the finding that low-income parents 'commonly prefer to sacrifice spending on themselves, rather than see their children go without'.

The report, by three Loughborough University academics, was based on a survey of 1,239 randomly-selected children.

___

As many as 85 per cent of mothers say they sometimes go without clothes, shoes or holidays in order to provide for their children. One in 20 sometimes go without food . . .

___

It found that the cost of bringing up a child to the age of 17 is around £50,000. The annual costs include nearly £1,000 on food, £260 for clothes, £186 on schooling, plus £333 on Christmas and birthday presents.

The survey said: 'As many as 85 per cent of mothers say they sometimes go without clothes, shoes or holidays in order to provide for their children. One in 20 sometimes go without food to ensure their children have enough to eat.'

Critics said the research was wrong to claim from a survey that lone mothers and parents on benefit commonly make sacrifices for their children.

Institute of Economic Affairs sociologist Patricia Morgan said: 'I doubt whether parents really go without.

'At my local Post Office you see the welfare Sharons out every Monday morning buying Silk Cut in batches of 80. It is the first thing they do, along with buying the lottery ticket.'

© *The Daily Mail*
July, 1997

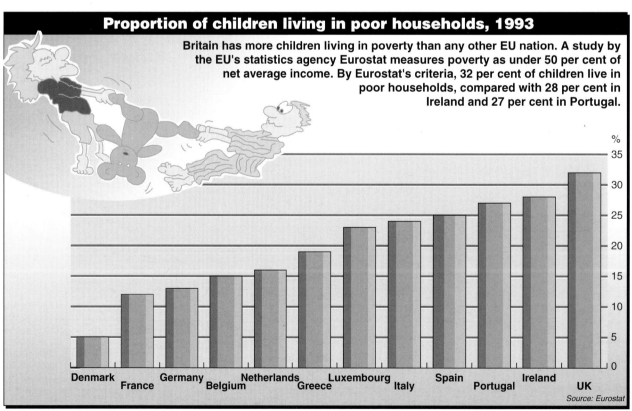

Proportion of children living in poor households, 1993

Britain has more children living in poverty than any other EU nation. A study by the EU's statistics agency Eurostat measures poverty as under 50 per cent of net average income. By Eurostat's criteria, 32 per cent of children live in poor households, compared with 28 per cent in Ireland and 27 per cent in Portugal.

Denmark | France | Germany | Belgium | Netherlands | Greece | Luxembourg | Italy | Spain | Portugal | Ireland | UK

Source: Eurostat

Families spring the poverty trap

Half of the poorest people in Britain work their way out of the poverty trap every year, a research group admitted yesterday.

Millions painted by the poverty lobby and left-wing politicians as mired in hopeless need in fact escape rapidly to a higher income level, the Rowntree Foundation said.

Two-thirds of those who climb out of the lowest income bracket manage to maintain their higher incomes, it added.

The conclusions throw fresh doubt on suggestions that 14 million people in Britain are poor – a claim repeated earlier this year in work sponsored by the foundation. Rowntree's past reports on poverty have angered Ministers and other critics, who accuse its researchers of being more concerned with equality than poverty.

The new research suggests millions fall into money difficulties when they lose a job or a marriage or live-in partner. Their circumstances then rapidly improve when they find new work or a new partner.

Those who stayed poor were mainly single pensioners or families with children where the parents were not working, the charity said yesterday.

The new findings are based on work by the Research Centre on Micro-Social Change at Essex University, which has studied the lives of 7,900 people over several years.

The foundation says: 'By following the same people over time, the research casts important new light on year-to-year changes in disposable income. These changes are not apparent from Government statistics.'

It adds: 'Finding paid work was a common reason for people moving above the level of low income. Unemployment, the arrival of a new baby, the death of a partner and divorce were important reasons for households falling below the threshold.'

Professor Stephen Jenkins of the Essex research centre said: 'The research reveals considerable variation in the incomes of individual families from year to year. But the picture that emerges is of a churning of incomes rather than a one-way ticket out of poverty.'

> ## The conclusions throw fresh doubt on suggestions that 14 million people in Britain are poor

A Rowntree report on poverty in 1995 was dismissed as exaggerated by Social Security Secretary Peter Lilley. This summer a follow-up document from the charity called for a payment of £15 a week to poor families to save them from going hungry.

That report was launched in tandem with the Channel 4 Poverty Commission, sponsored by the TV company, which this month recommended higher taxation and control of 'fat cat' salaries to help the poor.

The poor were said to include anyone on an income of under around £19,000 a year.

- Forty-eight per cent of those on low incomes in 1991 – below half the average household income – had climbed out of the 'poor' group by the next year.

- Fewer than a quarter of the low-income group stayed there for four years from 1991 to 1994. Only four out of ten below the 'poverty line' in 1991 were still there in 1994.

- Only one in ten of those interviewed for the study had stayed in the 'poor' bracket for three years or more. One in three fell below the line at some time during the three years.

© The Daily Mail
October, 1996

Poverty linked to deaths

By Sarah Ryle

Britain's poorest children are five times more likely to die in an accident than those from the richest households, according to a leading charity, which today accuses politicians from all parties of ignoring the most crucial issue in their campaign to win voters on education.

Child poverty has tripled since the Conservatives came to power in 1979 and the fresh analysis by the Child Poverty Action Group (CPAG) showed the poorest are also at greater risk of accidental death than they were in 1987.

British poverty levels, affecting 4.2 million children, compared to 1.4 million in 1979, are the worst in the European Union after Portugal and Ireland and CPAG says it is nation-wide.

The difference in accidental death rates had risen as income inequality has grown – poorer families are aware of the risks but are less able to make their environment safe for children.

Ministers and shadow ministers on the campaign trail yesterday traded blows over teaching standards and school league tables, but CPAG said they were missing the point.

The Conservatives now promise league tables for seven and 14-year-olds, and Labour has proposed homework clubs, improved technology and smaller classrooms.

But CPAG's director, Sally Witcher, said: 'While assessment tests are all the rage, the poverty that blights the chances of so many children is quietly ignored.'

Her organisation issued targets for the new government: reduce child poverty by half; guarantee a childcare place for one in four children aged under eight; halve the annual 227 poverty-related deaths among children; and halve the number of homeless children.

CPAG called for much of the previous 18 years' legislation squeezing housing, benefits and schools to be reversed.

© *The Guardian*
March, 1997

The causes of poverty

Information from Church Action on Poverty

Causes

The causes and effects of poverty are often complex and deeply personal. Each individual has their own experience and it is vital that their own voice is heard. A number of broad issues can, however, be identified.

Unemployment – In 1979 there were just over 1 million people out of work. The official total now is around 1.6 million, although the real level is much higher. In November 1996 the Government revealed that there are 2.1 million people who are unemployed and looking for work, but not claiming benefit. In addition the number of part-time employees had grown by around 1.5 million since 1992.

Social Security benefits – The fact that benefits are uprated in line with prices rather than wages has reduced their effectiveness. In addition there have been many changes, including the elimination of a number of social insurance benefits and reductions in entitlement. Two particular reforms which have caused major difficulties are the introduction of the Social Fund (mainly repayable loans rather than grants) and the withdrawal of benefits from unemployed 16 and 17-year-olds. The introduction of Incapacity Benefit and Jobseeker's Allowance have cut benefits even further.

Income Support is not enough to live on. Research has suggested that a basic budget, providing only basic essentials, for a family of 2 adults and 2 children costs £36 per week more than they receive in benefits.

Taxation – Between 1985-95 the overall impact of tax changes reduced net incomes of the poorest 10% by an average £3 per week, whilst the richest 10% gained £31.50.

Poor housing and homelessness – An increasing problem for those on low incomes. The emphasis in recent years on owner-occupation – currently around 70% of homes are privately owned – has meant an underinvestment in homes for rent and a corresponding decrease in the availability of decent accommodation for those who cannot afford to buy. In Britain last year over 400,000 people were officially homeless.

© *Church Action on Poverty*

Booming Britain's millionaires break all wealth records

By Richard Woods

Booming Britain is turning the rich into the super-rich, creating more billionaires and multimillionaires than ever before. In the latest guide to wealth in Britain, published today by *The Sunday Times*, 16 people emerge as billionaires – six more than last year.

The top 500 in the new list, which has been expanded to include 1,000 entries, saw their wealth increase by 23% in a year. Those 500 are now worth more than £86 billion.

The surge in wealth has been fuelled by soaring asset prices and bull markets. Dr Philip Beresford, who has compiled the register for nine years, said: 'Asset prices are at all-time highs. The stock market has been roaring ahead and company profits are strong, giving them the liquidity to buy other companies at fancy prices.'

Property and land are also increasing in value: prime agricultural land can now command up to £5,000 an acre in some areas, a rise of 40% in the past year.

However, 'old money' and the landed gentry have declined further as a proportion of Britain's wealth. Only 155 of this year's top 500 inherited their money. In 1989, when the list was first compiled, more than half had inherited wealth.

Propelled to the top of the new list is Joe Lewis, 50, a former restaurateur who has become king of the currency markets. Born in his father's pub in the East End of London, Lewis now lives in the Bahamas, where he is estimated to have amassed £3 billion.

Mohamed al-Fayed, the owner of Harrods, the London department store, who is embroiled in allegations of sleaze against Conservative MPs, also emerges as a billionaire. Following years of uncertainty over his finances, he joins the list after his former rival, Tiny Rowland, who examined Fayed's business closely, endorsed his inclusion.

Bubbling just under billionaire status is another new entry, David Bromilow, a quiet accountant worth £800m. Much of his fortune comes from a stake he bought in Adidas, the sports goods company, when it ran into difficulty. After the company's revival Bromilow sold part of his holding for £427m and kept shares now worth more than £200m.

> ## The top 500 in the new list saw their wealth increase by 23% in a year

Unlike the 1980s, the boom reflected in such deals has not been accompanied by ostentatious displays of wealth. Many of the new super-rich remain low-key. One such is Barrie Haigh, a pharmacist who set up Innovex, a drug consultancy business, in 1979. Last year he sold it for £550m to an American rival. Haigh received about £275m from the deal, but refuses to make any public comment on his remarkable success.

Haigh easily counts among the seriously rich, but the qualifying level for this accolade has more than quadrupled in less than a decade. The top 200 had a minimum £20m in 1989; by 1993 that had risen to £50m; by 1995 it was £60m. To join the elite now requires at least £95m.

As well as land and stocks, art and entertainment markets are also brisk. While Lord Lloyd-Webber with £550m and Sir Paul McCartney with £420m are the richest entertainers, Noel and Liam Gallagher of the rock bank Oasis join the list with £40m. Nick Faldo, the golfer, enters it with £50m.

The bulk of the wealth creation that has taken place in Britain has come from a new climate of entrepreneurial endeavour. Also joining the list is Mark Dixon, who left school at 16 and started selling hamburgers.

In 1988 he sold his concern and used the proceeds to launch another company, Regus, which provides a range of fully serviced offices to blue-chip businesses. Today it has clients in 34 countries and Dixon, 37, is worth £250m.

Wealth and the elderly

The elderly inherit, not the meek, as thrift leads to record number of millionaires

By Steve Boggan

The meek are not inheriting the earth – the elderly are. According to new research into the distribution of wealth in the United Kingdom, one in 550 adults is a millionaire, and the fastest-growing group are pensioners.

More than 81,000 people are now classed as millionaires, the most in history, and, for the first time, the number who have grown rich by graft and thrift has overtaken those who have inherited wealth.

The research, by Datamonitor, a strategic management consultancy, shows that the number of millionaires – people with net, unencumbered assets over £1m and £50,000 in liquid assets – has more than doubled since 1991 when the figure stood at 31,100.

More than 19,000 of those are over 65, but only 17,000 out of the total of 81,000 inherited their money.

'This shows a major shift in wealth reflecting people's concerns about providing for themselves in their old age, rather than relying on state provision,' said Harsha Yogasundram, an analyst at Datamonitor.

'People are saving more and investing more, a trend which is resulting in the elderly having more spending power than before.

'People who inherit their money still form a large proportion of millionaires, but it is a shrinking proportion.'

Datamonitor's figures, gleaned from public records at the Inland Revenue, the Central Statistical Office and the Office of National Statistics, show that in 1991, 8.2 per cent of millionaires were elderly – over 65 – compared with 9.5 per cent who were inheritors.

By 1995, the balance had shifted to 19.1 per cent elderly and 16.8 per cent inheritors.

Of all millionaires, 24 per cent are elderly, almost 21 per cent inherited their wealth and 12 per cent saved it from highly paid employment. Last year, of the 10,000 new millionaires, 2,000 were elderly, 1,200 were inheritors and 810 were workers.

> *The number of millionaires – people with net, unencumbered assets over £1m and £50,000 in liquid assets – has more than doubled since 1991 when the figure stood at 31,100*

There is also a small, but increasingly significant, group who have gained their wealth through the National Lottery. By the end of 1996, there were 288 lottery millionaires; the figure now is nearer 300.

The research does not, however, look at the strikingly obvious – the fact that more millionaires at the top must equate to more poor people at the bottom.

Datamonitor is preparing new research on what it calls the 'middle bracket' of earners, those with £10,000 to £100,000.

However, asked whether a third piece of research would be forthcoming on the poor, Datamonitor said no. 'There's not much call for that,' said Mr Yogasundram.

Just as well. The price for a copy of the latest report, *UK High Net Worth Individuals* 1997, is £1,495.

Kids really, really want to be rich

Modern children are shameless materialists who value wealth above health and happiness, according to a survey out today. Asked to name one wish, 40 per cent of the 7- to 14-year-olds polled by Fox Kids television network wanted to be rich, while only 4 per cent sought happiness and 4 per cent health.

The survey of more than 1,000 youngsters across the country found they hanker after the top designer labels, big houses, cars and televisions, and the Spice Girls are their top role models. Making money was the main aim in life among 38 per cent of the teenage boys surveyed, and 16 per cent wanted to win the lottery.

Half the boys said life would not be worth living without football and nearly as many – 47 per cent – found television essential to life. They reeled off Calvin Klein, Ralph Lauren and Armani as their favourite designer labels in clothes, and Adidas, Nike, Kickers and Reebok in footwear. Fox Kids managing director Rod Henwood said: 'Kids today are increasingly adopting adult values and our challenge as a children's channel is to create a kids' world that entertains without corrupting them.'

Lottery winners find out that money can't buy happiness

Simon Midgley finds instant wealth has turned many ordinary people into losers

Winning huge sums of money does not buy you love, it seems, let alone happiness.

Yesterday three-times married Mark Gardiner, 33, appeared to be continuing a tradition of big lottery winners whose backgrounds are tending to distract from the fact that they have won millions of pounds.

Mr Gardiner, joint winner with Paul Maddison of Saturday's record lottery jackpot of £22.6m, was the focus of a media scrum after being criticised in the *Sun* by both his estranged third wife and his adoptive mother. The latter, Irene Cresswell, was quoted as saying: 'I hope he drinks himself to death with his money.'

Since the first National Lottery draw on 19 November last year, 60 people have become millionaires, of whom about 15 have agreed to publicity. Mr Gardiner is the latest in a line to have tested the resources of Camelot's publicity machine to the fullest.

After the previous biggest winner, Mukhtar Mohidin, won £17.8m in December last year he squabbled about the windfall with his family and friends, Mr Mohidin, 44, a factory worker from Blackburn, then decamped south to a £375,000 mansion in the Home Counties, changed his name and obtained a legal order banning the identification of himself or his three children. He was condemned by leaders of his local mosque who said it was against the law to gamble and in April his friend, Ismail Lorgat, threatened to sue him for half his win claiming he had put up half the stake.

In May, a row over money at a family reunion led to him bundling several relatives into a car and driving to Amersham police station where they were held for several hours before being released without charge. On Sunday, the *News of the World* reported him as saying: 'I've been pissed off since I won . . . I don't like people now.'

In March, Lee Ryan, 32, a jobless father of three from Leicester, won £6.5m with his partner, Karen Taylor. It later transpired that he is to stand trial for the alleged theft and handling of stolen cars.

Since the first National Lottery draw on 19 November last year, 60 people have become millionaires, of whom about 15 have agreed to publicity

---

One of the earliest winners of the lottery, Lynn Turner, a 38-year-old shop assistant from Byram, West Yorkshire, who won £1,760,966 with her mother, said she would have given it all away if she could have saved the life of her brother-in-law who later died of cancer.

Camelot offers winners the services of two independent financial advisers and two independent legal advisers for at least five years after their wins. It also has four other winners' advisers who advise more generally about things like how to handle relatives, begging letters and the publicity. What none of these advisers can do, however, is change human nature or guarantee that wealth will bring happiness.

In the very first draw last November, George Snell, 69, won £839,254 with his daughter, Tricia Marden. Camelot laid on a press conference to reveal the identity of some of the winners. A grumpy Mr Snell delayed its start by half an hour after arriving late, refused to pose for the photographers and eventually stalked off to a nearby bar until the event was over. There's no pleasing some folk.

© *The Independent*
June, 1995

World poverty

Why the world's poor are getting poorer

At the millennium's end there is much to celebrate. Former colonies are free, fewer people suffer from polio, and apartheid is dead.

Yet one in five of the world's people still live in dire poverty. So that an African baby is seventeen times more likely to die before its first birthday than a British baby.

But it need not be like this. The world has the wealth and the means to end poverty.

Britain's richest ten people have as much wealth as 23 poor countries with over 174 million people.

Throughout the Third World people are taking on their governments, often risking their lives in the struggle for freedom and food. But unless they are supported by changes in rich countries, injustice will continue.

For people are made poor by decisions taken by governments, banks and companies in rich countries. So unfair are these decisions – on debt and trade, on weapons and policies – that money is actually passing from the poor countries to the rich.

The World Development Movement (WDM) is campaigning for new policies to tackle the major causes of world poverty.

The poor are getting poorer

In 1960 the richest fifth of humankind had 30 times more wealth than the poorest fifth; now they have 60 times more.

Debt crisis

In just one year, half a million children died from worsening poverty as poor countries strained to repay their debts.

In the 1970s, rich countries' banks and governments lent huge sums to the Third World. As interest charges soared, countries have paid back more than they borrowed – and yet are deeper in debt.

In 1995, for every £1 given in aid, rich nations took back £3 in debt payments.

To keep up the payments, Third World governments have slashed spending. Many African countries now spend more on their debts than on health. Which is why diseases once eradicated are coming back, like yellow fever in Ghana.

As former Chancellor Kenneth Clarke said: 'Energetic action on debt would make a radical difference to the prospects of many of the poorest countries in the world – at no practical cost to creditor countries.'

Many loans went to the military. Yet when people have overthrown the generals, their democracies are undermined by the burden of debt.

Men Sta Ana, campaigning in the Philippines for the cancellation of corrupt loans made to the Marcos dictatorship, says: 'These loans did not help people. They were used to suppress people and to abuse human rights.'

Economic strait-jackets

To survive, poor countries go cap-in-hand to the World Bank and the International Monetary Fund (IMF) which lend money only if countries adopt harsh economic programmes, including cuts in basic services.

So Zimbabwe, on the brink of achieving secondary schooling for all, started charging for education and health. Since when, more children have dropped out of school – and in the capital, Harare, the number of women dying in childbirth has doubled.

Throughout Britain, thousands have joined WDM's campaign, urging their bank and the Government to cancel poor countries' debts.

Trade

When you buy a £1 bar of plain chocolate, the British Treasury gets more (15p) than the cocoa farmer (8p).

People everywhere want to work. And poor countries earn eight times more from trade than aid. To create jobs and tackle poverty, they need to sell more. But the structure of world trade puts a lid on how much they can earn.

The Third World has four-fifths of the world's people but only one-fifth of its trade.

Rich countries sell expensive manufactured goods while paying little for natural products like cocoa from the Third World.

Poor countries cannot sell more manufactured goods because rich countries put barriers in their way. For example, Europe strictly limits clothes from poor countries – but lets in any amount of clothes from the rich world.

Barriers to textiles and clothing alone cost the Third World £35 billion a year in lost trade – as much as all Western aid.

Yet if poor countries could earn their way by selling more, they could buy more British goods, boosting jobs here.

Giant corporations

In Nigeria, the Ogoni people are demanding compensation from oil giant Shell whom they accuse of destroying their land and health. The Nigerian military hanged Ken Saro-Wiwa and eight other activists and over a thousand people have been killed during the campaign.

All countries depend on transnational corporations (TNCs) to invest in factories and services which create jobs. But TNCs play one country off against another to get the best tax breaks, cheapest materials and most lax labour laws. So little wealth stays in poor countries.

So vast are these corporations, they can dictate the world trade rules and escape national laws.

The explosion of Union Carbide's factory in Bhopal in India killed thousands. After a ten-year battle in the courts of two countries, only 4% of victims have received any compensation.

But consumers and public opinion can influence corporate thinking. For example, a survey of US bankers found that almost half had stopped lending for environmentally sensitive projects.

WDM is campaigning for multinational companies to clean up their act and for governments to tighten controls over TNCs.

Arms sales and conflict

Roberto Kafala was tortured by electric-shock batons supplied to the Zairean police by British businessmen. He says: 'I do not understand why the people of the West use their expertise to make this kind of technology. Why can't you sell us something useful?'

At the root of many wars is poverty, deepened by unfair trade and the debt crisis. Rich nations could help end the suffering. Instead they pursue military strategies and arms sales which prop up repressive regimes, increase tensions and prolong conflicts.

Britain is the world's second largest seller of arms, and four-fifths of British arms sales are to the Third World.

When sanctioning arms exports, the Government claims to take account of human rights. Yet Britain still arms Indonesia which, since invading East Timor, has killed 200,000 people.

In fact, the Government gives more support to arms manufacturers than other exporters. Every day the Government pledges £5 million of taxpayers' money to back arms exports. If the buying country does not pay up, the taxpayer shells out for the arms. Which is why the taxpayer is

giving £652 million to bankers and arms sellers left with Saddam Hussein's unpaid bills, including for military supplies.

Sam Cummings, international arms dealer says: 'You elect the Government and you support it with your taxes, a large percentage of which goes for weapons . . . Is there any basic difference between me and each of you?'

At the same time as filling countries' arsenals, the West is training its own guns on the Third World. To justify their high bills, the military points to drug barons, fundamentalists, even refugees, as threats to the West's wealth and security.

Britain's share of research money for the European Fighter Aircraft could eradicate polio worldwide and write off ten African countries' debts.

Redirecting resources into tackling poverty and backing useful exports could create jobs at home, meet poor people's needs and make the world safer.

WDM has exposed how taxpayers' and bank-customers' money is backing arms sales, even to repressive regimes.

Aid

In Burkina Faso, in a project supported by aid, women farmers built stone banks to save water and stop the soil washing away. In this way they reclaimed degraded land and dramatically increased their harvests.

The poor do not want to depend on aid. But it can help countries deal with sudden crises and build up their economies. And aid to community groups can open new opportunities.

Yet only four rich countries have fulfilled the UN target of giving 0.7% of national income (GNP) in aid. Indeed most are cutting aid. By 1995, Britain was giving only 0.28% of GNP in aid.

What is more, most aid is not spent in the poorest countries – or on meeting people's basic needs. Britain is one of only four donors to reduce aid to Africa between 1980 and 1885.

According to the UN, only 6p in every £1 of British aid goes on basic needs such as clean water or primary schooling.

Instead, aid is spent helping British business. On average 66p in every £1 of aid is given only if the poor country uses it to buy British.

Such aid favours big high-tech schemes, like dams, over small-scale solutions, like local wells. It traps countries into importing spare parts, and undermines local companies who need this business.

Blood from a stone

LOAN DEPT.

Eurodad – the European Network on Debt and Development – a Brussels-based umbrella group including Christian Aid, Cafod and Oxfam – has undertaken the first country-by-country survey of the main creditor nations.

What poorer countries pay back to the UK

Net transfer on debt, US$m

Source: EURODAD

Moreover according to a government study, one such scheme, the Aid and Trade Provision, delivers: 'very few real economic benefits for the UK economy'.

Worse still, aid is sometimes linked to winning arms orders. Globally, Third World countries with high military spending are rewarded with more aid, and strategic allies are favoured over the poor.

After the Gulf War, European Union aid to Egypt, an ally, rose 400%.

WDM is campaigning for a better-funded aid programme that benefits poor people in poor countries.

Campaigns get results

'There is no doubt that in 1992 the campaign of letters orchestrated by the World Development Movement, supported by the other agencies, prevented the aid budget from being cut,' said Mark Robinson MP, Private Parliamentary Secretary to the aid minister.

All these policies – on debt, trade, arms sales and aid – can be changed. As a taxpayer, voter and customer, you can help influence the Government, the European Union, the companies and the banks. And you can help win the policy changes which directly help the world's poor.

Acting in solidarity

Our Government, large multi-national businesses and our banks knowingly make decisions which keep people in the Third World poor. It is up to us to demand change – now.

Every day people in the Third World are fighting to stop the injustice of poverty. Their means are limited, their voices often stifled. It is vital that we support them.

This briefing explains the major global forces which combine to keep people poor – and how WDM is campaigning for change.

Your voice counts

In 1994 WDM won a High Court battle, proving that the Government's use of aid money for the Pergau Dam in Malaysia was illegal.

The money was promised by Ministers keen to clinch an arms sale to Malaysia. £200 million of aid money was saved. Some of this has now been used to clear landmines in Cambodia and for emergency aid to Rwanda and Bosnia.

In 1995 WDM, working with organisations in Asia and the UK, put pressure on toy companies to adopt a health and safety charter to improve working conditions in toy factories world-wide. The success of the campaign was due to the support of WDM's members, ready to act and join forces with other groups world-wide.

WDM has achieved many such major changes which have directly benefited the poor. With your help we can achieve more.

Acting for change – join WDM

WDM campaigns for political changes to bring justice for the world's poor by tackling the root causes of poverty.

We are a membership organisation and rely on the support and action of people like you.

WDM:
- works together with people in the Third World

- is aligned to no political party but influences all

- is a democratic network of members, groups and campaigners

- wants your support to help stop poverty

WDM members receive regular action updates, up-to-date information, and our bi-monthly newspaper.

Join WDM. Help us bring justice for the world's poor.

© World Development Movement
January, 1997

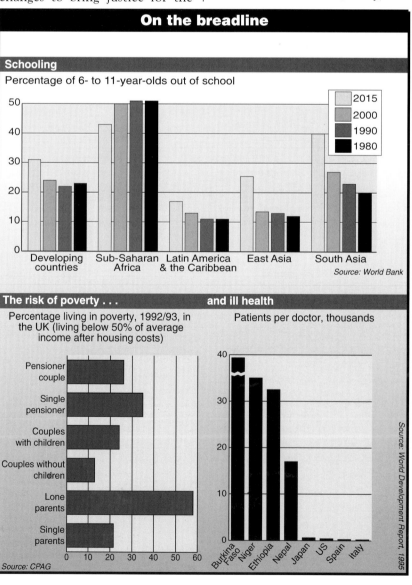

On the breadline

Schooling

Percentage of 6- to 11-year-olds out of school

Source: World Bank

The risk of poverty ...

Percentage living in poverty, 1992/93, in the UK (living below 50% of average income after housing costs)

Source: CPAG

and ill health

Patients per doctor, thousands

Source: World Development Report, 1995

Bridging the poverty gap

A projection of world poverty trends to the year 2000

Bridging the poverty gap

'Looking back over the last 21 years, it is clear from the advances made that absolute poverty is ultimately eradicable. The efforts of governments, donors and charities as well as poor people themselves have resulted in enormous strides in improving the incomes and livelihoods of thousands of people.

'But progress for many is being undermined by the increasing numbers of people who are being left behind. These people make up the growing global underclass, a group for whom there has been little or no improvement over the last two decades.

'The widening gulf between developed and developing countries is increasingly mirrored by the sharp divide between the burgeoning global underclass and developing countries themselves. If action is not taken now to bridge this gap then the millions who exist in grinding poverty will continue to slip through the net.'

Martin Griffiths
Director, Actionaid

To mark its 21st anniversary, ACTIONAID has compiled this analysis of world poverty.

During the last 21 years, substantial improvements in the quality of life for many of those in absolute poverty have been achieved. This clearly demonstrates that poverty and human hardship can be defeated.

But looking ahead there are worrying signs that the very poorest people are falling further behind. For the millions of people who form the global underclass, poverty is on the increase.

The global underclass

During the last two decades, the proportion of people in poverty has declined although the numbers in absolute poverty have increased. The majority of these people have seen very little improvement or have actually seen earlier gains disappear. One in five people in developing countries can now expect to live in extreme poverty, subsisting on less than 50 pence a day.

Poverty has become much more regional. During the last decade, the incidence of poverty increased in Latin America, where incomes have dropped by ten per cent, and in Sub-Saharan Africa, where incomes have fallen by 20 per cent. Within countries, the gap between rich and poor has also increased. The number in poverty in rural areas has increased by 40 per cent over the last 20 years.

Poverty has become much more focused on specific groups. Increasingly, the burden of poverty has fallen on those least able to bear it – women, children, ethnic minorities, those who are ill, disabled and landless. For example, the number of women in absolute poverty has almost doubled over the last 21 years.

It is these people – those for whom regional averages and national trends mask a downward spiral into poverty – who make up the emerging global underclass.

It is these people – those for whom everyday life is a struggle for existence – who provide the greatest challenge to policy makers worldwide as we approach the end of the

millennium. Tackling absolute poverty on this scale will require a massive global effort – but it is achievable.

Even under the most optimistic forecasts, however, prospects for the global underclass will remain bleak unless action is specifically directed to address their needs. For example, the prospect for Sub-Saharan Africa under one scenario – based on a four per cent growth rate, higher than that achieved over the last decade – is that the numbers of those in absolute poverty will more than double from the current 184 million to around 304 million by the turn of the century. Reversing these trends must be a major priority for the world community.

'Children in the Least Developed Countries are almost twice as likely to die before the age of one than the average among all developing countries.'

Meeting basic needs

Dramatic strides in the immunisation of children, over the last 21 years, now mean that more than three million lives are being saved every year according to UNICEF. However, despite this progress, 24 children still die needlessly every minute of every day from three preventable or treatable diseases – pneumonia, diarrhoea and measles. The majority of these occur in the Least Developed Countries (LDCs) where 30 per cent fewer children under one are immunised compared to developing countries in total. While it is likely that partial immunisation for more children will be achieved by the year 2000, the impact on the health of the poorest children will be limited if their basic needs are not adequately met.

Meeting the basic needs of people in absolute poverty must be the central development goal. This must include provision for health care, increasing incomes, food security, safe water, shelter, adequate sanitation and education. Donor countries must ensure that aid programmes are effectively targeted at meeting basic needs. In 1988-89, for example, only 8.8 per cent of British aid (latest available figures) was directed at basic education,

primary health care, safe drinking water, family planning and food security. ACTIONAID would like to see this increased to 20 per cent at least over the next seven years. As well as redirecting development resources, the amount of aid must also be increased to meet the needs of the growing number in absolute poverty.

'From today to 1 January 2000, 87 million children will die from preventable diseases at the current rate.'

Trade

Since the early 1970s, the prices paid for developing countries' primary exports have declined by over 20 per cent. Over this period, Sub-Saharan Africa's share of trade has shrunk by almost three-quarters to a mere one per cent of world trade. This compares to 19.3 per cent for developing countries as a whole. The outlook over the next seven years depends, to a large extent, on the outcome of the GATT Round negotiating the reforms necessary to enable poor countries to improve trading relationships. Trade links are vital for developing countries – trade produces six times more income for poor countries than aid. Allowing developing countries access to markets in industrial countries by removing barriers, specifically on agricultural and textile products, would help to boost export earnings which can then be used to tackle poverty. Industrial countries could also examine new mechanisms to stabilise world prices for primary commodities.

Donor countries and institutions should not insist on increasing production of primary commodities under structural adjustment agreements as this leads to over-production and falls in commodity prices.

Debt

During the last 20 years, the amount of debt owed, as a proportion of the value of exports from developing countries, has almost doubled. Servicing this debt costs developing countries around $170 billion annually – roughly equivalent to Belgium's annual national income.

The major impact of debt burdens is felt most keenly in Sub-Saharan Africa and Latin America, where it paralyses and disfigures national economies and blocks much-needed expenditure on human development. During the last 20 years, debt service, as a proportion of exports for the LDCs, has increased by 450 per cent compared to an increase of just 75 per cent for all developing countries. Total debt owed in Sub-Saharan Africa is equivalent to virtually the whole of its national wealth.

A number of innovative debt reduction schemes during the last decade have helped to highlight the problem of developing countries in debt. However, this focus has not resulted in a significant reduction in the debt burden faced by many developing countries.

Full implementation of the Trinidad Terms by the Paris Club is necessary if developing countries are to begin to reduce debt payments. A planned programme of write-offs for debt-distressed countries, alongside encouragement for private creditors to do likewise, would enable poor countries to free up funds for economic and social development. Until the burden of debt is eased, developing countries will have insufficient funds for investment in poverty reduction.

Conflict

During the last two decades, conflict in developing countries has increased dramatically. Bitter ethnic wars continue to rage, bringing famine and disaster to civilian populations. The end of the cold war, the difficult move to democracy in many countries and the rise of clan and ethnic divisions within countries, as well as poverty itself, suggest that the prospects for new conflicts occurring in many parts of the world are high.

The last few years have witnessed increasing demands on the international community for humanitarian interventions as war and poverty have taken their toll. Only 13 of the 47 LDCs enjoyed basic peace and stability over the last decade.

Conflict exacerbates poverty and environmental degradation and reduces the available resources for long-term development. The world community should strengthen mechanisms to prevent conflict arising in the first place and enable humanitarian assistance to be balanced against the principle of sovereignty. At the moment, particularly in countries such as Somalia and Ethiopia, assistance from the international community is often too little, too late.

Enhancing the role of the UN must involve adequate financing to ensure that it can carry out its mandate.

Environment

Over the last two decades, enormous and largely unchecked damage has been wrought on the environment. Some 480 billion tonnes of topsoil – roughly equivalent to the amount of India's cropland – were lost due to environmental degradation over the last 20 years. Between 1973 and 1988, some 1,450,000 sq. km of forest were cleared – roughly equivalent to six times the area of Britain – for non-agricultural purposes. Efforts to reduce environmental degradation are unlikely to match the increasing pressures on the natural environment over the next seven years. It is the poorest people, who rely more than any other group on the natural environment, who suffer the greatest consequences of environmental degradation. Reducing environmental degradation and enabling poor countries to develop in a way that minimises environmental damage is a huge challenge for policy-makers. Donor nations must fully integrate environmental concerns into their aid programmes and must make available appropriate technologies. Reducing absolute poverty will help significantly to reduce damage to the environment. Rich countries could also review their own consumption patterns.

Population

During the last 21 years, 1.6 billion people have been added to the world's population – more than inhabited the world in 1900. The projection (UNFPA) for the year 2000 is for an extra billion people to be born. The prospect, by 2050, is that ten billion people will inhabit the world. Such rates of increase depend on real progress being made on giving access to family planning facilities and reducing family size.

Poor people currently have little or no choice over the number of children they have. An estimated 300 million couples lack access to the services they need to plan their family size.

The poorest countries (LDCs) have a population growth rate 50 per cent higher than that of all developing countries – in the late 1980s, 25 LDCs had a population growth higher than that during the 1970s – and contraceptive use is more than 70 per cent lower.

Rapid population growth can be a critical factor in hindering efforts to reduce poverty. Tackling rapid population growth should involve strategies to improve the livelihoods of poor people, enabling them to have a real choice over the size of their families and creating the conditions in which this choice can be exercised.

Education

Although illiteracy rates in the developing countries dropped from 48 per cent in 1970 to 34 per cent in 1990, during the same period the actual number of illiterate people in those countries rose from 731 million. Primary school enrolment has increased in recent decades, but the challenge set out in the 1990 UN Jotien 'Education For All' conference – of full enrolment by the year 2000 – already seems to have been forgotten, as other priorities grab the headlines and government budgets. Spending per head on education among the 37 poorest countries has fallen by a quarter over the past decade. Particularly alarming is the fact that, whereas in 1970, 59 per cent of illiterate people in developing countries were women. In 1990, 60 per cent were women. Donor countries should ensure that primary education is retained as a priority, and that within this a greater focus is placed on primary education for girls and adult literacy for women, in order to prevent this gender gap from widening over the coming years.

- 1.1 billion people – a fifth of the world's population – live in absolute poverty
- The gulf between the very poorest and other developing countries has widened
- Between 1 and 1.5 billion people will live in absolute poverty by the end of the decade

• The above is an extract from *Bridging the Poverty Gap*, a briefing produced by Actionaid. See page 41 for address details.

© Actionaid
March, 1993

FANCY STARTING A POVERTY TRAP?

Poverty in Europe — living below the line

The figures released on 15 May 1997 by the statistical office of the European Union concerning the number of people in poverty in twelve of the fifteen member states for the year 1993 are mind-boggling. Unfortunately they only confirm what the members of the European Anti Poverty Network know too well from their daily experience. According to the Eurostat figures, there were over 57 million individuals living in nearly 23 million poor households. For some countries, there was a staggering increase during a period of five years (between 1988 and 1993).

Poverty lines

The poverty line is defined in relative terms: a person is considered poor if she/he has a net monetary income below 50% of the average income in her/his country. The poverty line can be shown either in national currencies or in 'Purchasing Power Parities'. The Purchasing Power Parities (PPPs) convert every national monetary unit into a common reference currency of which every unit can buy the same amount of goods and services across the countries in a specific year. This conversion enables international comparisons.

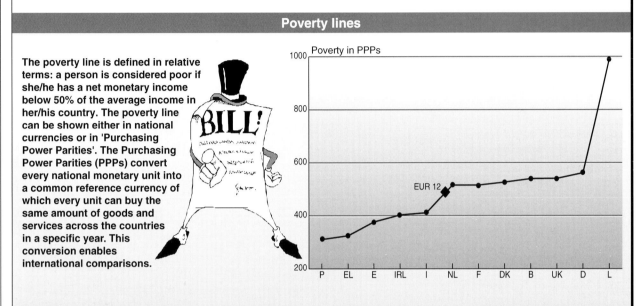

The extent of poverty in 12 European countries

A household with an income lower the the poverty line (see above) is defined as 'poor'

This table gives an indication of the increase in poverty between the late eighties and 1993. The figures cannot be strictly compared as the statistical base is different; however, they give an indication of the trend.

Country	In the late Eighties Individuals living in poor households %	1993 Individuals living in poor households %	1980s -1993 Increase %
DK	4.3	6	44.5
D	11.9	11	23.5
B	9.4	13	38.9
NL	4.8	13	171.8
F	16.5	14	-17.9
L	11.5	15	42.8
I	22.0	20	-13.7
E	17.7	20	11.3
IRL	19.4	21	10.5
EL	20.5	22	10.1
UK	15.3	22	46.8
P	25.1	26	2.2
EUR 12	14.9	17	10.0

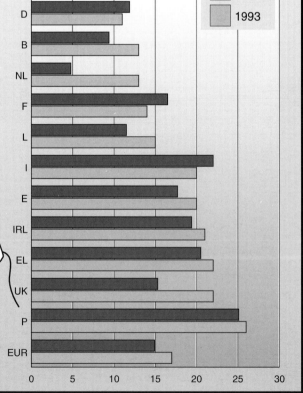

The poor by household type

Representing 19% of the total, the most common profile of poor households was that of a person living alone and aged over 65 years. Couples without children also formed a significant portion at 18%, while couples with at least one child aged 16 or over comprised 13% of this category. Some types of households are 'poorer' than others. As measured by the poverty rate, it is evident that the poverty risk was much higher for 'single parents with all children under 16' than for 'couples with one child under 16', 36% versus 11% in 1993.

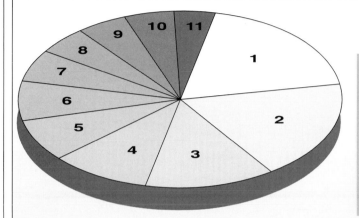

Key:

1	One person aged 65 or over	19%
2	Couple without chilren	18%
3	Couple with at least one child>16	13%
4	One person aged 30-64	10%
5	Couple with two children <16	8%
6	One person aged under 30	7%
7	Other households	6%
8	Couple with one child <16	5%
9	Couple with three children and more<16	5%
10	Single parent with all children <16	5%
11	Single parent with at least one child>16	4%

Poor households

Overall, the proportion of poor households in the UK is ranked third from the bottom at 23 per cent, compared with Greece at 24 per cent. The EU average is 17 per cent, and again Denmark has the lowest levels of poverty, with just 9 per cent of households in the poverty line bracket.

Proportion of poor households		Proportion of children under 16 in poor households	
Denmark	9%	Denmark	5%
Germany	13%	France	12%
Belgium	15%	Germany	13%
Holland	14%	Belgium	15%
Luxembourg	14%	Holland	16%
France	16%	Greece	19%
Italy	18%	Luxembourg	23%
Spain	19%	Italy	24%
Ireland	21%	Spain	25%
UK	23%	Portugal	27%
Greece	24%	Ireland	28%
Portugal	29%	UK	32%

Source: Poverty, Child Poverty Action Group (CPAG)

GDP per head

Comparisons are for 1994, latest available. They are in PPS (Purchasing Power Standards). GDP per person is not the same as disposable income. So these figures don't necessarily mean people in one region are more prosperous than in another. Commuters can boost the GDP of the region where they travel to work and thus reduce it where they live.

Regions above 1.5 times EU average	
Hamburg (Germany)	196
Brussels (Belgium)	183
Darmstadt (Germany	178
Ile de France	161
Oberbayern (Germany)	161
Vienna (Austria)	158
Bremen (Germany)	156
Hessen (Germany)	152

Note: The data do not split Luxembourg into regions. But, taken as a country, it is near the top of this table at 169. PPS is used to cancel the impact of price differences among countries by using a common reference currency of which every unit can buy the same amount of goods and services.

Regions below half EU average	
Voreio Aigaio (Greece)	49
Azores (Portugal)	48
French overseas departments	45
Ipeiros (Greece)	43

Source: European Anti Poverty Network

Exploding the myths about poverty

There's a lot said about poverty that's misinformed, prejudiced or just downright offensive. Myths about poverty are extremely damaging. They distract us from the most important question: in a society as prosperous as ours why are people not protected from hardship? To have that debate we need to get the facts and figures straight. Being able to distinguish fact from fiction is where to start.

Some people say that poverty doesn't exist in the UK. They look around and see no swollen-bellied, bare-footed children and conclude that no one is starving and that there are only poor people in Africa, not here.

'Poverty doesn't exist in the UK'

But poverty does exist here in the UK. There are people going without sufficient food and warmth, with people so desperate that they need to take to the streets to beg for food. And freedom from poverty isn't only about basic survival; it also means being able to participate in society, rather than merely exist. Latest figures show there are more than 14 million people living in poverty in the UK. In a society as rich as ours it is a crime that so many have such poor quality of life.

'How can they be poor – they've all got videos!'

Some people do not have access to basic amenities – tables, chairs and beds – let alone videos. But more than three-quarters of the population do have video recorders, including some people living in poverty. If you were living on a low income could you afford to go to the cinema? It's often cheaper to rent a video. Being in poverty isn't only about what you have and haven't got, it's also about being able to have a normal social life like going to a cinema every once in a while.

'It's not like it was in my day – there isn't really any poverty in the UK today'

Some people remember the poverty of the 1930s and argue that poverty no longer exists. Being poor in the 1990s isn't the same as being poor in the 1930s – some essential modern appliances weren't even invented then. Poverty changes according to the society and the time in which you live.

'The poor don't want to work, they're lazy and expect wages which are too high'

Some people fortunate enough to have work think that those in poverty should 'get on their bikes' and pull themselves out of their situation. They think that people living in poverty are an 'underclass' who don't want to work or won't work because they don't think they'll be paid enough. But people in poverty come from all walks of life and include the young and old and those in and out of work. To dismiss poor people as 'an underclass' is both meaningless and offensive.

Those that argue that there are plenty of jobs out there for those lay-abouts scrounging off the taxpayer perpetuate a myth that there are a large group of unemployed people who are happy to depend on benefits. Unemployment, however brief, causes hardship and trauma and people who are unemployed speak of experiencing a loss of dignity and shame.

Most of the unemployed want to work. They often have difficulty finding a job because there simply aren't any jobs around. Where there is work, it is often so low paid that it doesn't meet the extra costs which workers face, such as travel costs, childcare and clothing. It's a fact that some people are better off not accepting a low-paid job. And when jobs are increasingly insecure – offering 'zero-hour' contracts or low-

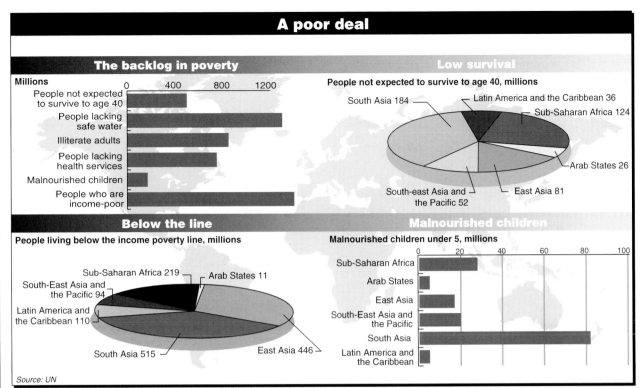

A poor deal

The backlog in poverty

Millions

- People not expected to survive to age 40
- People lacking safe water
- Illiterate adults
- People lacking health services
- Malnourished children
- People who are income-poor

Low survival

People not expected to survive to age 40, millions

- South Asia 184
- Latin America and the Caribbean 36
- Sub-Saharan Africa 124
- Arab States 26
- East Asia 81
- South-east Asia and the Pacific 52

Below the line

People living below the income poverty line, millions

- Sub-Saharan Africa 219
- Arab States 11
- South-East Asia and the Pacific 94
- Latin America and the Caribbean 110
- South Asia 515
- East Asia 446

Malnourished children

Malnourished children under 5, millions

- Sub-Saharan Africa
- Arab States
- East Asia
- South-East Asia and the Pacific
- South Asia
- Latin America and the Caribbean

Source: UN

---

paid temporary work – the risk in taking employment is greater. It's often women who find themselves in the poverty trap but men are increasingly caught in the trap too.

'Benefit levels are adequate to live on'

Some people think it's easy to live on benefits – even luxurious! They point to the price of baked beans and sliced bread and claim that benefits offer easily enough to live on, and more. But research has shown that benefit levels are unquestionably meagre and do not meet the costs of even a modest budget. They provide no scope for many necessities, such as a winter coat or children's shoes. As a result people are forced into debt or have to go without for the sake of their children.

'Poverty is caused by lone parenthood'

Some people have claimed that the payment of social security benefits has led to the breakdown of the family, arguing that young women get pregnant so they can get a council house and live off the state.

Poverty is not caused by lone parenthood but by factors associated with it: the difficulty of finding employment with suitable working hours that also covers childcare costs and the inadequacy of benefits to meet the extra costs associated with being a lone parent. Benefits are not generous enough to act as an incentive for lone parenthood. Rather than scapegoating lone parents, they need support to help them into work and to meet the basic costs that come with having a family.

'Foreigners come here to scrounge off our social security system'

The term 'benefit tourism' has been used to describe great numbers of people from abroad supposedly coming to the UK in order to claim social security benefits. There is no evidence to support this claim. In fact, some refugees enjoyed much better standards of living at home than they could hope to do here. The UK has extremely strict regulations preventing people from abroad from claiming benefits – so much so that they are preventing people with legitimate claims from getting the benefits they deserve. It's shameful that a country as affluent as ours shuts its doors to those desperate for refuge.

'Benefits are for poor people – rich people should not be entitled to any benefits'

The social security system was set up for everyone. It is not a system exclusively for the poor. Many benefits are not income-related. For example you are entitled to a pension or child benefit under certain conditions, regardless of your level of income. These sorts of benefits are important because they can prevent poverty from occurring in the first place. Income-related benefits, on the other hand, only provide support once poverty has struck, they are stigmatising, have a low take-up, are expensive to administer and create 'poverty traps' which act as a disincentive to moving into work or increasing income.

'I've worked hard for what I've got, I'm damned if I'm going to share it!'

Everyone – rich and poor – has a stake in the social security system because anyone could find, given certain circumstances, that they need to rely on others for support.

Changes in taxation have benefited the rich more than the poor. In particular those on low incomes have lost out through the growth of indirect taxation – such as VAT – because they pay a higher proportion of their income on such taxes than rich people. Tax cuts, such as the decrease in the higher rate of income tax, have especially benefited the rich.

'The poor haven't got poorer'

Some say that because people spend more nowadays, they can't be poor.

Differences in the spending levels of the rich and poor have increased since 1979 but not to the same extent as income. This does not mean that the poorest 10 per cent are no longer poor. Many people who fall into poverty are forced to run down savings or get into debt.

Some say the poor haven't got poorer because those in poverty now are not necessarily the same people as were poor before. Others argue that it's OK to have poverty because the poor are never poor for very long. There is little information on how people's incomes change or how long people spend in poverty. But comparisons over time reveal that as a group the poorest 10 per cent in 1979 were poorer in 1992 in real terms, even if they were not the same individuals. A quarter of the population now lives in poverty, a dramatic increase since 1979. The experience of poverty, however short-lived, is traumatic. Attempts to play down the extent of poverty should not be allowed to overshadow the unacceptability of the very existence of poverty in an affluent society.

'There's no such thing as poverty, only inequality'

Some people argue that what 'poverty' refers to is really 'inequality'. Inequality certainly exists and there is a close relationship between poverty and inequality. But poverty is not the same as inequality: it is possible to have an unequal society which has no poverty.

Some argue that it's OK to have inequality, even desirable in a market-driven, capitalist society. They believe that economic growth helps everyone because wealth trickles down to the poor. Others suggest that even if inequality is not desirable, it will never be eliminated – some people are just better at managing their money than others.

CPAG believes the extraordinary growth of inequality in the UK scars our society and must be reversed. There is evidence throughout the world that 'trickle down' does not work. Despite rising average incomes, a recent drop in unemployment and evidence of increasing ownership of consumer goods, the gap between the rich and poor has grown ever wider, with those at the bottom losing out.

Cuts to benefits and changes in taxation have increased the gap between the rich and the poor. Inequalities in our society are linked to such things as ill health and crime; we would all benefit from a more equal society.

'We need to cut back on social security expenditure'

Some people say that the social security bill has grown to over £90 billion because benefits have become more generous or because they have been paid to people who don't deserve them. And yet some benefits have decreased in value and many people who need benefit are still going without support.

Others argue that our ageing population means we face a 'demographic time bomb' which threatens to explode social security expenditure. But the UK's population has already aged more rapidly than in other European countries – the time-bomb should have already detonated!

Some have blamed the increased spending on social security on massive amounts of benefit fraud. While fraud can never be condoned it is important to put it in perspective.

The amount lost in benefit fraud is exceeded by the huge sums lost in unpaid tax each year.

While any substantial rise in public expenditure should be of concern, the UK does not spend as much as many other European countries on social security. Benefit spending has risen because of the growth of unemployment and the impact of policy decisions (such as subsidising rents via housing benefit rather than investing in bricks and mortar). Increasing employment opportunities and recognising the impact that decisions made in and outside the Department of Social Security have on social security expenditure are more likely to reduce spending.

'The poor will always be with us'

Some people will always have less than others but that does not have to mean there will always be people living in poverty. It should be our primary aim to achieve a society where all people can freely participate and attain a decent standard of living. The UK is still a wealthy nation. No society as rich as ours should be complacent about its level of poverty. It is possible to eradicate poverty if there is a will to do so.

© CPAG

Women and poverty

- More than one-fifth of the global population lives in extreme poverty (*The World Health Report 1995*)

- The number of rural women living in poverty nearly doubled over the past 20 years. Today women constitute at least 60% of the world's billion rural poor. (UN publications. 1994. DP1/1424)

- Poverty has increased by 48% among rural women over the past 20 years, compared with only 3% among rural men. (*Report on Rural Women Living in Poverty*. IFAD. 1992)

- Between 10 and 40% of female-headed households live in poverty. (*Women in a Changing Global Economy*. UN.1995)

- One-third of families world-wide are headed by women. (*The World's Women: 1970-1990. Trends and Statistics*. UN. 1991)

- One in five households is headed by women in 74 developing countries. (*Report on Rural Women Living in Poverty*. IFAD. 1992)

Compiled by WOMANKIND Worldwide

Women left chained to agriculture and poverty

The World Food Summit opens in Rome tomorrow aiming to find a way of halving the world's undernourished people in the next two decades from 840 million. For entirely practical reasons, reports John Hooper, those concerned with food aid development regard the female of the species as their priority

In the heady days of the 'Green Revolution', recalls Marie Randriamamonjy, foreign development workers devised a scheme to plant high-yielding rice in west Africa. The chosen variety had an unusually short stalk. Time went by, but the size of the harvests failed to increase.

'Then they found out that it was not the men, but the women, who did the harvesting. The women went into the fields with babies strapped to their backs, and harvesting the rice had become almost impossible for them because the new strain was so close to the ground,' says Ms Randriamamonjy, of the UN's Rome-based Food and Agriculture Organisation (FAO).

One of the more striking aspects of the frequently opaque declaration to be adopted at the FAO-sponsored World Food Summit, which begins in Rome tomorrow, is the emphasis on the role of women. On the very first page, heads of state and government are called on to acknowledge the 'fundamental contribution to food security by women'.

This has little to do with political correctness. For entirely practical reasons, development workers increasingly see women as their priority targets.

The International Food Policy Research Institute has said that 'income in the hands of women contributes more to household food security and child nutrition than income controlled by men,' according to a study published last year.

The director of the FAO's women and population division, Leena Kirjavainen, said she reached a similar conclusion during her years as an educational adviser in Sudan.

'If money is given to women, it is generally used for better nutrition, better clothing, and for the welfare of the household. If it's given to men, it tends to be spent on electronic goods, a new bicycle maybe, or – if we're to be really frank – on prostitution, alcohol and other forms of consumption that don't help the family.'

The World Food Programme (WFP), another UN body based in Rome, insists that 80 per cent of its food aid be given directly to households, usually through the senior female member.

Ironically, since women and girls are believed to account for seven out of ten of the planet's hungry, it is they who produce much of the food. Latest estimates put the proportion of 80 per cent in Africa and 60 per cent in Asia, much higher than development workers had thought.

The level seems to be rising. As men migrate to the cities, the world

- World's poorer countries still need aid and support on vast scale.

- 40 per cent of the population of Sub-Saharan Africa is chronically undernourished.

- Summit declaration, agreed by officials, commits the world to halve the number of undernourished people by 2015.

- Forecast global cereal production seven per cent higher than in 1995. Production of rice also forecast to rise.

- Sub-Saharan Africa is producing less food per person than it did 30 years ago.

is seeing a process which Dr Kirjavainen calls 'the feminisation of agriculture and poverty'.

Women often lack the education needed to cope with their new responsibilities. Two out of every three illiterates in the world are women.

There is thus an increasing strong belief that, in the long term, the best way to feed the world's poor will be to educate its women. The WFP's director in Pakistan, Peter Jobber, began putting that idea into practice with a scheme to give families a can of cooking oil for every month each of their daughters spent at primary school.

'Fairly typically in the more conservative, rural areas, only about a quarter of the girls are even enrolled. Actual attendance can be as low as 5 to 10 per cent,' he says.

The WFP targeted Baluchistan and Frontier Province – poor, arid regions along the borders with Iran and Afghanistan, where purdah is the norm.

'In two years we have doubled enrolment, and the attendance of the girls who are enrolled has increased to 95 per cent,' says Mr Jobber.

He believes the success of the programme suggests these areas are 'not as conservative as outsiders think'. He encountered little resistance on grounds of religion or tradition. Parents had been keeping their girls away for financial reasons – to help with work at home. When the balance of economic advantage was tipped in the opposite direction, they became enthusiastic supporters of their daughters' education.

© The Guardian
November, 1996

World's top 10 billionaires

1

William Henry Gates III – Wealth: $18 billion
Listed by Forbes business magazine as the richest man in the world, Gates, 40, founded Microsoft, the world leader in PC software, with school friend Paul Allen (see below). Now chairman and chief executive.

2

Warren Buffett – Wealth: $15.3 billion
Chair of investment, insurance and holding company Berkshire Hathaway, Buffett, 65, also has 10 per cent stake in American Express. Nicknamed the Sage of Omaha because of astute investment decisions.

3

Paul Sacher – Wealth: $13.1 billion
Now 90, Swiss Sacher was appointed honorary member of the board of pharmaceuticals giant Roche after standing down at recent AGM.

4

Lee Shau Kee – Wealth: $12.7 billion
Based in Hong Kong, Asia's richest man is chairman of Henderson Land and Henderson Investment.

5

Tsai Wan-Lin – Wealth: $12.2 billion
Founder of Taiwanese insurance empire Cathay Life.

6

Li Ka-Shing – Wealth: $10.6 billion
Chairman of Cheung Kong (Holdings) Ltd and Hutchison Whampoa Ltd made his fortune by building up property around his Hong Kong plastic flowers factory. Major donor to the Conservative Party, with strategic stakes in 20 listed companies, some controlled by Chinese mainland corporations. Hutchison Telecommunications is doing well in Hong Kong, as is the group's involvement in the Asiasat satellite project and Star television service.

7

Yoshiaki Tsutsumi – Wealth: $9.2 billion
Once listed as the world's richest individual but the Tsutsumi fortune has halved since 1987 because of falling Japanese property values.

8

Paul G Allen – Wealth: $7.5 billion
Co-founder and second biggest shareholder of Microsoft Corp. Has stakes in several software, on-line, entertainment and sports companies.

9

Kenneth R Thomson – Wealth: $7.4 billion
Son of the late Lord of Fleet, the chairman of Thomson Corp owns newspapers world-wide and has moved into electronic publishing. Also owns Hudson's Bay Company.

10

Tan Yu – Wealth: $7 billion
Head of real estate empire stretching from the Philippines, Taiwan and China to San Francisco, Las Vegas and Houston. Left school at 13 to work as baggage boy in Manila, made his first million at 17, selling T-shirts.

© The Guardian
April, 1996

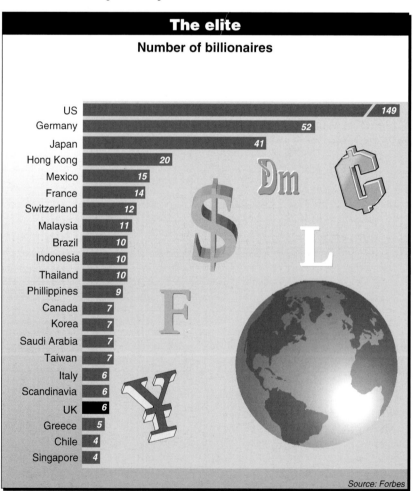

The elite

Number of billionaires

US	149
Germany	52
Japan	41
Hong Kong	20
Mexico	15
France	14
Switzerland	12
Malaysia	11
Brazil	10
Indonesia	10
Thailand	10
Phillippines	9
Canada	7
Korea	7
Saudi Arabia	7
Taiwan	7
Italy	6
Scandinavia	6
UK	6
Greece	5
Chile	4
Singapore	4

Source: Forbes

Ted Turner gives $1bn to the poor on a whim

By Charles Laurence in New York

Ted Turner, the media entrepreneur who founded CNN, has given $1 billion to the United Nations in the biggest single charitable donation on record.

'It's going to go to the poorest people in the world, the people who need it most,' he told guests at a dinner in New York held to benefit the UN's support organisation.

He said later that he had thought of the gift while reading a monthly statement of his wealth two days before his speech.

The statement had revealed that he had made $1 billion in the past nine months – his wealth rising from $2.2 billion to $3.2 billion.

'I only got the idea 48 hours ago . . . on the spur of the moment, like buying a new car,' he said. 'I'm only giving up nine month's earnings. It's not that big a deal.'

The gift comes five months after he made a speech castigating America's wealthiest for being 'ol' skinflints', calling on them to give more to charity and demanding that the nation learns to measure personal prestige not by wealth accumulated but by wealth given away. He singled out Bill Gates, chairman of Microsoft, and investor Warren Buffett, America's richest men with $15 billion each, as men who should give away $1 billion.

He accused the Forbes 400 list of the richest Americans of 'destroying our country'.

His theory is that the list keeps tycoons from giving money away because they might slip down the list and lose face 'at the yacht club'.

Mr Turner, 58, who is married to Jane Fonda, the film star, was number 46 on the Forbes list a year ago. The merger with Time Warner was to have raised him up into the top 25.

The announcement of the gift, which will benefit children, refugee aid, the clearing of land mines and the prevention of disease, came as Mr Turner was making a speech in acceptance of an award for Global Leadership, in recognition of the impact of his CNN cable news and his campaigns for the environment and human rights.

> **'I only got the idea 48 hours ago . . . on the spur of the moment, like buying a new car. I'm only giving up nine month's earnings. It's not that big a deal'**

His money will go to the United Nations in the form of a special fund receiving $100 million, mostly in stock, each year for 10 years. Mr Turner, the winner of the 1977 America's Cup and the 1979 Fastnet Race, has bought vast tracts of land in the West, from Montana to New Mexico. He is the biggest private landowner in the country with 1.3 million acres.

His holdings include the Atlanta Braves baseball team and the Atlanta Hawks basketball team. The whole empire was built from a billboard company he inherited and a local radio station he bought to exploit a more modern form of advertising.

Known as The Mouth of the South – his home base remains Atlanta, Georgia – he has said that Christianity is 'for losers'. When he told his wife, a devotee of radical causes, what he had done, it 'brought tears to her eyes', he said. 'She said, "I'm proud to be married to you," and I never felt better in my life,' he added.

Describing our world in the 90s

Information from the Catholic Fund for Overseas Development (CAFOD)

Different terms are used to describe the economic divisions of our world: rich and poor, developed and developing. Until recently, First, Second and Third World were commonly used, but these terms are more political than economic and refer to who has power in the world.

Maps influence the way we see the world. The Peters Projection shows all countries on the same area scale. Compared with the more usual projections, European countries appear to have 'shrunk' and the countries nearer the equator seem to have 'grown'.

Because of the many changes of the 80s it now seems more appropriate to use the terms North and South to describe our world.

The North

The North includes North America, Europe, Japan, the Commonwealth of Independent States (formerly USSR), the oil-rich states of the Persian Gulf and also Australia. Most of the world's wealth and industry is concentrated in these countries.

The North has:
- 25% of the world's people
- 83% of the world's wealth
- 90% of the world's manufacturing industry
- 85% of the world's arms
- 87% of the world's energy consumption

People in the North can expect to live, on average, to over 70. Most people eat well and have a secondary-school education.

The North dominates the international economic system and the world's financial institutions.

The South

The South includes Africa, Asia, the Pacific, Latin America and the Caribbean. Not all people in these countries are poor; a small minority are very rich. (We exclude Australia and the New Zealand since economically and culturally these belong to the rich North.)

The South has:
- 75% of the world's people
- 30% of the world's food grains
- 17% of the world's wealth
- 11% of the world's education spending
- 6% of the world's health expenditure
- 30% of the people of the South cannot meet their basic needs for water, food and shelter.
- One-quarter of children die before they reach the age of five.
- Over one-third of the people suffer malnutrition
- Only about half the population receive any schooling at all.

Food for everyone

There is more than enough food grown in the world to provide everyone with an adequate diet. Considering grain alone, enough of this is produced to provide the world's whole population with sufficient protein and more than 3,000 calories per day. Yet according to the World Bank, 1.2 billion people, nearly a quarter of the world's population, are too poor to have a healthy diet and the number is growing. The problem is that much of this grain is in the over-supplied countries of the North.

Trade – a raw deal?

Trade is one of the strongest links between the rich, industrialised countries of the North and the poorer countries of the South. When the North had colonies in the South it wanted crops and raw materials which the South could supply cheaply like coffee, cotton, sugar, and rubber. This still happens, and

the South continues to buy the North's manufactured goods at far higher prices.

Profits go north

70% of this trade is done by large multinational companies based in the North. Often the same company can make large profits by doing the growing, processing, shipping and marketing of the crop.

Coffee is the second most valuable raw material, after oil, on the world market. More than 40 countries of the South grow it but almost all of it is processed in the North. Nestlé (Nescafé) and Philip Morris (Maxwell House) produce over three-quarters of the coffee drunk in the UK. Out of £1.50 paid for a jar of coffee in UK shops, only 12p will go to the coffee-bean picker in the South.

Declining prices

In 1990, the prices of raw materials allowing for inflation were generally lower than they were in 1980.

In Bangladesh the cost of a power-tiller in 1970 required 1.5 tonnes of raw jute.

To purchase the same power-tiller in 1992 required 9 tonnes

In West Africa the cost of a tractor in 1965 required 3 tonnes of bananas.

The same tractor in 1990 required over 20 tonnes.

Cash crops

In order to earn more (often to repay debts), countries of the South are pressured to grow less food for their own people and more cash crops for export: sugar, coffee, tea, cocoa, rubber and even flowers and strawberries.

Debt

In the 1970s banks in richer countries of the North had surplus money to lend. They encouraged poor countries of the South to borrow for development projects like building roads, dams, hospitals, schools, but sometimes for military purposes. By the end of the 70s, interest rates rose and the South needed more money to pay the interest on their loans. At the same time prices for imports rose and the price they received for their exports fell. They turned to the IMF

for help. But the IMF made further loans conditional on drastic austerity policies – cuts in government spending (often on essential services like health and education), devaluation, and abolition of food subsidies.

Tanzania is now using 96% of its export earnings for debt repayments.

Brazil's foreign debt amounts to $740 for every man, woman and child in the country.

In 1988 the debtor nations of the South transferred to the North over $52 billion more than they received in new loans, aid and investment.

Signs of hope

One of the signs of hope for the future is the continuing formation of thousands of development groups, basic Christian communities, human rights and justice groups in the countries of the South. CAFOD supports initiatives in the South which enable the poor to work together for a fairer world.

Things to do

1. Find out from your weekly shopping basket how much food comes from countries of the South. Look out for the Fair Trade Mark on goods in supermarkets and shops.

2. Find out about organisations like Traidcraft, Oxfam Trading, TWIN Trading and Equal Exchange to know what they are doing to create fair trading.

3. Support CAFOD in its development work with poor communities through Working in Partnership. Write to CAFOD for other Fact Sheets on topics like Trade, Aid and Debt. See page 41 for address details.
© CAFOD

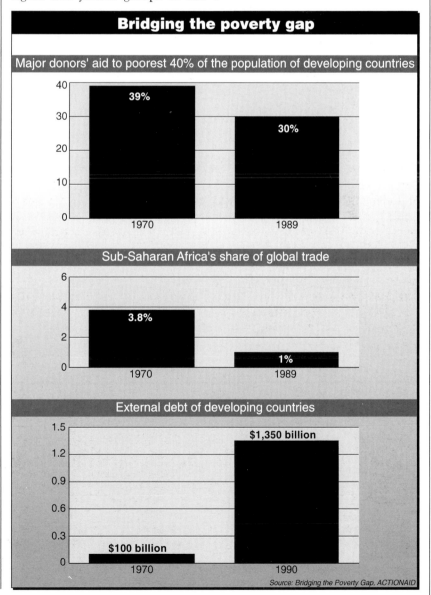

Bridging the poverty gap

Major donors' aid to poorest 40% of the population of developing countries

1970: 39%
1989: 30%

Sub-Saharan Africa's share of global trade

1970: 3.8%
1989: 1%

External debt of developing countries

1970: $100 billion
1990: $1,350 billion

Source: Bridging the Poverty Gap, ACTIONAID

World warned of poverty time bomb

Call for aid to be linked to good policies

By Larry Elliott in Hong Kong

The World Bank president, James Wolfensohn, put the fight against global inequality at the top of the development agenda yesterday with a stern warning to prosperous nations that they ignored the gap between rich and poor at their peril.

Pledging that the Bank had learned from its past mistakes, Mr Wolfensohn said: 'The time has come to get back to the dream: the dream of inclusive development.'

The president used his key-note speech at the annual meeting of the World Bank and International Monetary Fund to drive home to the West that without more equality there would be neither peace nor global stability. 'What we are seeing in the world today is the tragedy of exclusion. Whether you broach it from the social or the economic or the moral perspective this is a challenge we cannot afford to ignore.'

Mr Wolfensohn added that the objective was to reduce glaring disparities both within and between countries, thereby bringing more people into the mainstream. 'This – the challenge of inclusion – is the key development challenge of our time.'

Michel Camdessus, managing director of the IMF, also stressed the need for 'solidarity' and the 'responsibility of industrial countries to help minimise the social and cultural costs of integration into the global economy'.

Although the Fund's structural programme for Thailand is certain to cause economic hardship, Mr Camdessus said that the IMF was 'now raising the issues of income distribution in its ongoing dialogue with member countries and emphasising the need for greater equality of opportunity'.

Mr Wolfensohn, who has been battling to reform the Bank's internal structure while at the same time promoting debt relief for the poorest countries, said the privileged of the developing and developed world could close their eyes to what was happening.

'But we must recognise that we are living with a time bomb and unless we take action now, it could explode in our children's faces.

'If we do not act, in 30 years the inequalities will be greater. With population growing at 80 million a year, instead of three billion living on under $2 (£1.25) a day, it could be as high as five billion. In 30 years, the quality of our environment will be worse. Instead of 4 per cent of tropical forests lost since Rio, it could be 24 per cent.'

Outlining a programme for partnership development, Mr Wolfensohn said the governments and peoples of developing countries should be 'in the driver's seat' so they could set their own objectives.

It was also important for aid to be selective. 'There is no escaping the hard fact: more people will be lifted out of poverty if we concentrate our assistance on countries with good policies than if we allocate it irrespective of the policies pursued.'

He added: 'The message for countries is clear: educate your people, ensure their health, give them voice and justice, financial systems that work, and they will respond and they will save and they will attract the investment, both foreign and domestic, that is needed to raise their living standards and fuel development.'

Aid organisations, which in the past have been highly critical of the Bank's record, gave the speech a mixed response. Andrew Simms, of Christian Aid, said: 'There is a hell of a long way to go both on debt relief and on moving the World Bank into a position where it can achieve pro-poor economic programmes in the poorest countries.'

But Oxfam's Ian Bray said: 'We are extremely positive about Mr Wolfensohn's message. He set an agenda which is clearly focused on poverty reduction. That's what the Bank is going to be about.

'He sent a message to national governments that it is the coherence of policy – health, education and getting poor people into the economy – that will deliver poverty reduction, rather than big projects.'

© The Guardian
September, 1997

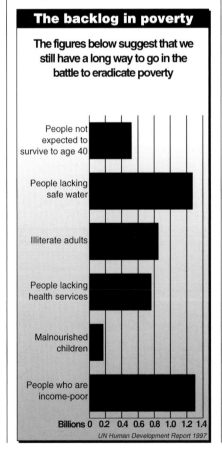

The backlog in poverty

The figures below suggest that we still have a long way to go in the battle to eradicate poverty

People not expected to survive to age 40

People lacking safe water

Illiterate adults

People lacking health services

Malnourished children

People who are income-poor

Billions 0 0.2 0.4 0.6 0.8 1.0 1.2 1.4

UN Human Development Report 1997

A world divided

Information from a summary of the *Oxfam Poverty Report*

Today, the world envisaged by the founders of the UN is at once more attainable and more distant than ever. The five decades which have elapsed since the UN was founded have witnessed some remarkable changes. Global economic wealth has increased sevenfold and average incomes have tripled. Parts of the developing world, notably East Asia, have significantly increased their share of world income. The record of advancement in human welfare, measured by increased life expectancy, falling infant mortality, improved nutrition, and increased educational attainment, has been unprecedented. Never before have the financial and technological resources for eradicating poverty been available in such abundance. Yet the world continues to tolerate levels of poverty and inequality which, by any civilised standard, represent an affront to morality, quite apart from a vast wastage of human potential. Cold facts and figures can never capture the extent of human suffering inflicted by the 'silent emergency' of poverty. But they do starkly illustrate the gulf between the world envisaged by the founders of the UN and present realities. In a period when technological frontiers are being pushed back at an unprecedented rate, we live in a world where:

- The richest fifth of the world's population, living in the industrially advanced countries, have average incomes thirty times higher than the poorest fifth.
- The poorest 50 countries, mostly in Africa, have seen their incomes decline to the point where they now account for less than 2 per cent of global income. These countries are home to one-fifth of the world's people.
- One in four of the world's people exist in a state of absolute want, with millions more living close to this perilous state.
- Poverty-related diseases claim the lives of 35,000 children every day.
- Half of the world's population is systematically discriminated against from the cradle to the grave for the 'crime' of having a female chromosome.
- Half a million women die each year from causes related to pregnancy and inadequate health care.
- 130 million children are denied the right to primary education; and the number of years which girl children spend in school is half that for boys.
- Approximately 1.3 billion people have no clean water or sanitation.

Poverty, inequality, and the growing gap between rich and poor are not confined to developing countries. In the United States an additional four million children fell into poverty during the 1980s, even though the wealth generated by the country's economy expanded by one-fifth. Governments in Europe have also failed to contain the drift towards deepening poverty and inequality.

The number of people living in poverty in the European Union grew from 38 million to 52 million between 1975 and 1988 and several countries experienced a dramatic increase in poverty and inequality. For example, until the mid-1970s, income inequality in the UK was in steady decline as economic growth increased general prosperity. Today, 12 million people live on less than half the average income, more than double the number in 1979; and the number of individuals living below the poverty line has increased from 5 million to almost 14 million.

Of course, poverty in the industrialised world is not the same as poverty in the developing world, being measured in terms of relative deprivation rather than absolute want. However, the willingness of governments in the world's richest countries to tolerate the exclusion of so many people from an acceptable way of life at home speaks volumes about a wider indifference to poverty.

- This text is based on a book published by Oxfam, *The Oxfam Poverty Report*. See page 41 for address details. *© Oxfam*

Brown speeds debt relief

Chancellor urges world financial leaders to accept tougher targets for helping poorest countries

The Chancellor, Gordon Brown, will this week spearhead a global initiative to cancel the debt of the majority of the world's poorest countries by the year 2000.

In his first major speech on development issues, to be delivered tomorrow to the Commonwealth finance meeting in Mauritius, Mr Brown will set a series of bold targets for speeding up the process of relieving poor countries of an estimated $5.6 billion (about £3.5 billion) of Western debt.

Mr Brown shares the growing view among churches and other development activists that the world's financial leaders need to inject new urgency into the process of easing debt burdens if it is not to seize up because of indifference and shortage of funding.

Despite high hopes for the initiative when it was launched last year, only one country, Uganda, has cleared the obstacle course put up by financial leaders, and even it will not benefit until early 1998.

Mr Brown is prepared to revive the campaign for sale of gold reserves held by the International Monetary Fund to ensure his new targets are met. Gold sales have been blocked by the German government.

Mr Brown will propose that by the millennium, 75 per cent of the world's poorest countries, most in Sub-Saharan Africa, will have in place schemes designed to cancel or relieve their debt with the IMF/World Bank and other official creditors. This will free domestic resources to invest in education, health and the relief of poverty.

Mr Brown will seek the support of the Commonwealth, and then the Group of Seven richest nations in Hong Kong on Saturday, for a number of proposals:

By Alex Brummer,
Financial Editor

- Poor countries with reform programmes in place, including a degree of transparency in their financial affairs and plans to expand production, should receive urgent relief.
- All creditor countries should follow Britain's example and cancel repayment of exiting aid loans.
- The official creditor's club which meets in Paris should be more flexible and go beyond the 80 per cent debt forgiveness proposed for countries like Mozambique.
- The World Bank should review the debt of the poorest countries to determine any gaps in debt relief not covered by existing plans.
- International financial leaders should look beyond existing plans to make sure the pressure is kept on for debt relief for all countries whose public spending is directed at production, rather than military spending or unnecessary prestige projects.
- Britain stands ready to provide technical assistance to countries which reshape their public finances and will urge other nations to do the same.

Despite the strong rhetoric from heads of government and financial leaders when the debt initiative was launched, it has been dogged by delays and bureaucratic snags.

The IMF, which is a full partner with the World Bank in dealing with the issue, has not been able to raise the cash to carry it forward.

Ironically, Mr Brown's plan will add to the IMF's cash needs by speeding up the process. However, the Treasury believes the additional pressure of targets will encourage countries to come forward with more resources and eventually lead to the freeing up of 5 million ounces of IMF gold for sale.

Finance ministers gathering in Hong Kong this week for the G7 and annual meetings of the IMF/World Bank will be told that four countries, Bolivia, Ivory Coast, Burkina Faso and Mozambique, are close to the point at which relief can be considered.

If the Brown target is accepted, 14 of the world's 19 poorest indebted countries should be on their way to debt relief by the turn of the century, paving the way for a new start in Africa.

The decision to set tougher targets is Mr Brown's first venture into the development area since taking over as Chancellor in May. He is picking up the baton of debt relief first carried by his predecessor, the Tory Chancellor Kenneth Clarke.

© The Guardian
September, 1997

Global poverty

Information from the United Nations Department of Public Information

The situation

Basic numbers

Of the 5.6 billion people on the planet, more than a billion live in a state of absolute poverty, with income and consumption levels below nationally defined poverty lines.

They are essentially bereft of life's basic necessities, struggling to survive on the equivalent of less than US $370 a year.

Some 550 million go to bed hungry each night. More than 1.5 billion lack access to clean drinking water and sanitation.

Life expectancy is short, a consequence of such factors as disease, hunger, malnutrition and crime. In Sub-Saharan Africa, people rarely survive beyond the age of 50, on average. In Japan, by comparison, the average is 80.

Education is virtually nonexistent. A billion adults are functionally illiterate, while some 500 million children have nowhere to go to school.

Who

The poor are in virtually every country, but the overwhelming majority are in the developing nations.

Women suffer disproportionately; they represent 70 per cent of the poverty-stricken population, followed closely by the elderly.

Infant mortality rates are about 175 per 1,000 live births in Africa and close to 100 in India; in the developed world, East and West, the average is about 15.

What

Poverty has been typically measured by the income or expenditure level that can sustain a bare minimum standard of living. But it is also a matter of such factors as nutrition, life expectancy, access to clean water and other aspects of human existence.

In terms of income levels, the World Bank has used an upper poverty line of $370 a year per capita as the cut-off; anyone below that is classified as poor. The very poor, by this definition, are those whose annual income equivalent falls below $275.

Where

The greatest concentrations of poor people are in rural areas of Africa and Asia.

Numerically, the largest number of severely impoverished people – about half of the total – live in South Asia, which is home to 30 per cent of the world's population.

Fighting poverty: the challenges ahead

The World Bank has recently announced that it will need to increase its efforts if it is to achieve its main aim of helping developing countries to reduce poverty.

Although the proportion of poor people in the world has declined, rapid population growth has meant that the number of people living on less than one dollar a day has increased from 1.23 billion in 1987 to 1.31 billion in 1993. This is more than one-fifth of the world's population.

Population living below US $1 a day in the developing world (1993)	Millions
East Asia and Pacific	445.8
Eastern Europe and Central Asia	14.5
Latin America and Caribbean	109.6
Middle East and North Africa	10.7
South Asia	514.7
Sub-Saharan Africa	218.6

© Worldaware

But they are most concentrated in Africa, particularly the Sub-Saharan nations. Although Africa has about 16 per cent of all world's poor, fully half all Africans are impoverished.

Although urban poverty continues to worsen, the rural poor still represent more than 80 per cent of the total number of poor people in the developing countries. Sixty per cent of the rural population of Sub-Saharan Africa lives in poverty, along with 31 per cent of the rural population of Asia. In Latin America and the Caribbean, 61 per cent of the rural population is poor, according to national estimates.

But poverty has also begun to swell in the developed countries; in the United States and Western Europe, nearly 15 per cent of the population lives below the poverty line.

The trends

Despite overall improvement in living conditions all over the world, poverty and inequality remain and appear to be worsening.

The World Bank has estimated that, if current trends continue, the number of poor people in the developing world alone could explode by 200 million by the end of the century.

This has highlighted the fact that poverty is a consequence not only of the misfortunes and limited capabilities of individuals but also of the structures and processes that determine the distribution of wages and salaries; the impact of various taxes and other public revenue sources at different income levels; land distribution, access to ownership and control of productive resources; and market price structures.

© United Nations Department of Public Information

Focus on aid

Information from the Overseas Development Administration

What is aid?

'Aid' is a term used to describe any type of assistance given to a country ranging from technical equipment and money to skilled workers and emergency supplies. There are many ways of giving aid.

Who gives aid?

Typically aid is given by rich countries to poorer ones in Africa, Asia and Latin America. However, since the collapse of the Soviet Union, some aid is now given to countries in Central and Eastern Europe and the former Soviet Union. Most aid is given by governments, either directly or through international organisations, but Non Governmental Organisations (NGOs) play an important role too.

Types of aid

Government to government aid
Bilateral aid
Government contributions to international organisations like the United Nations Children's Fund (UNICEF)
Multilateral aid

Aid from charities, churches and other civil groups
Non Governmental Organisation aid

Government aid (of all types)
Official Development Assistance

Why give aid?

Aid is given for a number of reasons. The main purpose is to reduce poverty and suffering and to help people in poorer countries to improve their lives. By making poorer countries stronger, aid can also make the world a more stable place with fewer wars and less discontent. It can also help preserve the environment. For instance, the poorer people are, the more likely they are to cut down trees for their own use or to sell. As

developing countries grow richer, they provide a boost to the world economy so all countries can benefit through increased trade.

Aid can also open up markets for British companies, particularly through the Aid and Trade Provision (ATP) which provides financial help to companies to enable them to compete for contracts in the developing world.

How can aid be spent?

Aid is spent on a variety of projects from building bridges and dams to providing short-term emergency food supplies and shelter after a natural disaster. Deciding how to spend money allocated as aid involves making difficult choices.
Here are some of the ways that £200 million could be spent:

- immunise 20 million children against the main six preventable diseases
- provide basic village-level water supplies to ten million people
- fund slum-improvement projects for over one million families
- build between 3,500 and 35,000 km of rural access roads

Aid from the UK

The United Kingdom ranks amongst the world's top aid donors. In 1993 the British government's Overseas Development Administration gave £1,948 million in Official Development Assistance, whilst British NGOs gave £302 million, £32 million of which came in grants from the government's Joint Funding Scheme (JFS). Nearly half of government aid went to Sub-Saharan Africa, the poorest region in the world, and nearly a third went on large-scale energy and infrastructural projects. While most people consider that providing aid for countries less well-off than ourselves is a worthwhile thing, others criticise the idea.

Advantages of government aid
- Its large size means that it can bring benefits to hundreds of thousands of people.
- Developing a poor country's industry and infrastructure can help to boost economic growth.

Criticisms of government aid
- Aid can help to create a more prosperous and less dangerous world.
- Quantity is not everything – not enough aid is targeted on the poorest sections of the population.
- Wealth rarely 'trickles down' to the rural poor, so those who benefit are mainly urban dwellers, particularly those who are already well-off.
- Some people argue that charity begins at home and that we should sort out our own problems before spending money on helping others.

• The above is an extract from *Global Eye*, published by Worldaware for the Overseas Development Administration. See page 41 for address details.

© *Global Eye*
Issue 1, Autumn 1996

ADDITIONAL RESOURCES

You might like to contact the following organisations for further information. Due to the increasing cost of postage, many organisations cannot respond to enquiries unless they receive a stamped, addressed envelope.

Actionaid
Hamlyn House
MacDonald Road
London, N19 5PG
Tel: 0171 281 4101
Fax: 0171 281 5146
Produces publications including reports, case studies and activity packs, multimedia, video packs, maps and reference books. Ask for their publications list.

Catholic Fund for Overseas Development – CAFOD
Romero Close, Stockwell Road
London, SW9 9TY
Tel: 0171 733 7900
Fax: 0171 274 9630
CAFOD is the official overseas development agency of the Catholic Church in England and Wales. They publish useful factsheets and information packs on the issue of poverty.

Child Poverty Action Group (CPAG)
Fourth Floor, 1-5 Bath Street
London, EC1V 9PY
Tel: 0171 253 3406
Fax: 0171 490 0561
CPAG seeks to ensure that families on low incomes get their full entitlement to welfare benefits and it campaigns for improvements in both benefits and other policies to eradicate the injustice of poverty. They publish a wide range of books and factsheets on issues relating to poverty, including *Poverty Magazine*.

Church Action on Poverty
Central Buildings
Oldham Street
Manchester, M1 1JT
Tel: 0161 236 9321
Fax: 0161 237 5359
An ecumenical organisation whose aims are to raise awareness about the causes, extent and impact of poverty in the UK. Produce publications on poverty.

Department for International Development
94 Victoria Street
London, SW1E 5JL
Tel: 0171 9170503
A wide range of information about the British aid programme, including the annual review of British aid, *British Overseas Aid*, is available free at the above address.

European Anti-Poverty Network
205 rue Belliard, Box 13
B-1040 Brussels, Belgium
Tel: (32) 2 230 44 55
Fax: (32) 2 230 97 33
EAPN is an independent coalition of non-governmental organisations (NGOs) and groups involved in the fight against poverty and social exclusion in the European Union.

Fawcett Society
45 Beech Street
London, EC2Y 8AD
Tel: 0171 628 4441
Fax: 0171 628 2865
Works to influence parliament and public opinion to accept equal status for women in the home and public life, and equal educational and job opportunities. They publish *Towards Equality*, a quarterly publication.

Help the Aged
St James' Walk
London, EC1R 0BE
Tel: 0171 253 0253
Fax: 0171 250 4474
Publishes information on many subjects surrounding ageing which is welcome for research enquiries.

Joseph Rowntree Foundation
The Homestead
40 Water End
York, YO3 6LP
Tel: 01904 629241
Fax: 01904 620072
The Foundation is an independent, non-political body which funds programmes of research and innovative development in the fields of housing, social care and social policy. It publishes its research findings rapidly and widely so that they can inform current debate and practice.

Low Pay Unit
27-29 Amwell Street
London, EC1R 1UN
Tel: 0171 713 7616
Fax: 0171 713 7581
Investigates low pay, poverty and related issues. Produces publications.

Womankind Worldwide
3 Albion Place
Galena Road
London, W6 0LT
Tel: 0181 563 8607/8
Fax: 0181 563 8611
Supports and raises funds for women in developing countries, works with them to overcome poverty.

World Development Movement
25 Beehive Place
London, SW9 7QR
Tel: 0171 737 6215
Fax: 0171 274 8232
Campaigns for policy changes which directly benefit poor people in the Third World. Produces informative leaflets on poverty-related issues.

World Vision
World Vision House
599 Avebury Boulevard
Central Milton Keynes, MK9 3PG
Tel: 01908 841000
Fax: 01908 841001
Produces magazine *World Vision*.

Worldaware
31-35 Kirby Street
London, EC1N 8TE
Tel: 0171 831 3844
Produces the publication *Global Eye*.

INDEX

in Wales 13
see also wages
inequality, and poverty 30
infant mortality rates 39
inner cities, and poverty 3

L
large families, and poverty 1
Latin America, poverty in 23, 24, 39
LDCs (least developed countries),
population growth rate 25
life expectancy
and global poverty 39
and social class 3
living standards, of rich and poor
people 3
London, wage levels 12
lone parents, and poverty 1, 2, 3, 7, 14, 27, 29

M
men, and unemployment 9
millionaires in Britain 17, 18
minimum wage 7, 11-12

N
National Insurance, and women in poverty 6
National Lottery winners 18, 19
North (developed countries) 34

O
occupational pensions 5, 7
Oxfam 36, 37

P
part-time work
earning from 12
regional variation in 12
and women in poverty 6, 7
pensions (retirement)
and the Retail Prices Index 4-5
and women 7
population growth, in developing
countries 25, 36
poverty
bridging the poverty gap 23, 35
causes of 2, 16
and elderly people 4-5, 7
in Europe 26-7
exploding myths about 28-30
people escaping from 15
risk of 22
and spending levels 29-30
statistics 1, 14, 26-27
poverty line, defining 26, 39

R
raw materials, price of 35
regional variations in poverty 3
retired population, and poverty 4-5
rich people *see* wealth
rural poverty 30, 31, 39

S
Scotland
government spending on 13
wage levels 12
self-employment, and poverty 11
single mothers *see* lone parents
social class, and poverty 3
social work, and child poverty 5
South (developing countries) 34
Soviet Union (former), aid to 40

T
taxation
and poverty 16, 29
and the retired population 16
Third World *see* developing
countries
TNCs (trans-national corporations) 20-1
trade, and developing countries 20, 24, 34-5
Turner, Ted 33

U
underclass
global 23-4
poor people as 28
unemployment
and men 9
and poverty 1, 2, 8, 10, 11, 15, 16, 28-9
and women 7
United Nations Convention on the Rights
of the Child 5
United States, poverty 39

W
wages
current wage levels 10, 12
minimum wage 7, 11-12
Wales
government spending on 13
wage levels 12, 13
WDM (World Development
Movement) 20, 21, 22
wealth
billionaires 32, 33
distribution of 20, 37
and the elderly 18
millionaires in Britain 17, 18
National Lottery winners 18, 19
women
in poverty 2, 6-7, 11, 30, 39
in developing countries 25, 31
World Bank 36, 38, 39
World Food Programme (WFP) 31

ACKNOWLEDGEMENTS

The publisher is grateful for permission to reproduce the following material.

While every care has been taken to trace and acknowledge copyright, the publisher tenders its apology for any accidental infringement or where copyright has proved untraceable. The publisher would be pleased to come to a suitable arrangement in any such case with the rightful owner.

Chapter One: The Poverty Trap
Poverty, © CPAG, *The price of a child*, © Joseph Rowntree Foundation, *The poverty debate*, © Help the Aged, *Children caught in poverty trap*, © The Independent, January 1997, *Poverty and financial security*, © The Fawcett Society, *Life on a low income*, © Joseph Rowntree Foundation, *Average spending on children*, © Joseph Rowntree Foundation, *Childhood poverty and parents' work*, © Joseph Rowntree Foundation, *Poverty and the minimum wage*, © Low Pay Unit, *Who are the poor?*, © Department of Social Security, *Millions would benefit from minimum wage*, © The Guardian, September 1997, *Low pay*, © New Earnings Survey, Office for National Statistics, Crown Copyright 1997, *Wales 'the poor relation' of UK*, © The Guardian, September 1997, *Employment*, © Joseph Rowntree Foundation, *The children of poverty*, © The Daily Mail, July 1997, *Proportion of children living in poor households*, 1993, © Eurostat, *Families spring the poverty trap*, © The Daily Mail, October 1996, *Poverty linked to deaths*, © The Guardian, March 1997, *The causes of poverty*, © Church Action on Poverty, *Booming Britain's millionaires break all wealth records*, © Times Newspapers Limited, April 1997, *Wealth and the elderly*, © The Guardian, February 1997, *Kids really, really want to be rich*, © The Independent, September 1997, *Lottery winners find out that money can't buy happiness*, © The Independent, June 1995.

Chapter Two: Global Poverty
World poverty, © World Development Movement, January 1997, *Blood from a stone*, © EURODAD, *On the breadline*, © World Development Report, 1995, *Bridging the poverty gap*, © Actionaid, March 1993, *Poverty in Europe*, © European Anti Poverty Network, *Exploding the myths*, © CPAG, *A poor deal*, © United Nations, *Women and poverty*, © Womenkind, *Women left chained to agriculture and poverty*, © The Guardian, November 1996, *World's top 10 billionaires*, © The Guardian, April 1996, *The elite*, © Forbes, *Ted Turner gives $1bn to the poor on a whim*, © Telegraph Group Limited, London 1997, *Describing our world in the 90s*, © CAFOD, *Bridging the poverty gap*, © Actionaid, *World warned of poverty time bomb*, © The Guardian, September 1996, *The backlog in poverty*, © United Nations, *A world divided*, © Oxfam, *Brown speeds debt relief*, © The Guardian, September 1997, *Global poverty*, © United Nations, *Fighting poverty: the challenges ahead*, © Worldaware, *Focus on aid*, © Overseas Development Administration.

Photographs and Illustrations
Pages 1, 8, 34: Andrew Smith, pages 3, 15, 23, 28: Michaela Bloomfield, page 6: Katherine Fleming, pages 17, 19, 25, 33, 37: Ken Pyne.

Craig Donnellan
Cambridge
January, 1998